Consul Willshire Butterfield, Historical Society Western Reserve

History of Brulé's discoveries and explorations, 1610-1626

Consul Willshire Butterfield, Historical Society Western Reserve

History of Brulé's discoveries and explorations, 1610-1626

ISBN/EAN: 9783337156848

Printed in Europe, USA, Canada, Australia, Japan

Cover: Foto ©ninafisch / pixelio.de

More available books at **www.hansebooks.com**

HISTORY

OF

BRULÉ'S DISCOVERIES
AND EXPLORATIONS

1610-1626

Being a Narrative of the Discovery, by Stephen Brulé, of Lakes Huron, Ontario and Superior; and of his Explorations (the First Made by Civilized Man) of Pennsylvania and Western New York, also of the Province of Ontario, Canada

With a Biographical Notice of the Discoverer and Explorer, who was Killed and Eaten by Savages

"The dauntless woodsman, pioneer of pioneers, Étienne Brulé, the interpreter." — PARKMAN

BY

CONSUL WILLSHIRE BUTTERFIELD

Author of "Crawford's Campaign Against Sandusky;" "Washington-Irvine Correspondence;" "History of the Discovery of the Northwest, by John Nicolet, in 1634;" "History of the Girtys;" and other works

THE HELMAN-TAYLOR COMPANY
CLEVELAND, OHIO
1898

PREFACE.

Few, if any, of the early events properly belonging to the pages of American history are of more interest and importance after the discovery of the New World than are those relating to the journeyings, the explorations, and the discoveries of Stephen Brulé. What this daring Frenchman accomplished in the (then) inhospitable wilds of what is now the northern portion of our country, and in the southern and western parts of the present Dominion of Canada, has not hitherto been given in detail by any historian.

Brulé was essentially a woodsman: his fondness for savage life was remarkable. But he wrote nothing; and his verbal recitals, as they were taken down from his own lips, and recorded by Champlain, Sagard and Le Caron, are not calculated to awaken at once the thought that they border on the marvelous. However, as we contemplate more and more his courage and perseverance among the Indian nations which he visited and with some of which he lived several years, our curiosity gives way to admiration and astonishment.

The date when Brulé flourished is, in our annals, an early one. He left France, his native country, and arrived in the valley of the St. Lawrence the next year after the English first gained a foot-hold in North America; and he started upon his journey with the savages, which resulted in the first exploration ever made westward of the great river of Canada and in the discovery of Lake Huron, ten years before the landing of the Pilgrims on Plymouth rock. And it was only six years after Henry Hudson first saw the river which bears his name that the subject of our narrative stood upon the shores of Lake Ontario — the first of civilized men to gaze out upon that broad expanse of water. It was but three years subsequent to the time when Manhattan island, now New York City, was first settled that he was, before any other white man, threading his way through the dark woods of what is now Western New York and soon after floating down the Susquehanna river in the present State of Pennsylvania,— reaching, finally, along the Chesapeake bay, the shore of the Atlantic ocean.

During the next decade, Brulé, having first visited a copper mine on the north coast of Lake Huron, advanced to his greatest triumph — the discovery, as it is believed, of Lake Superior. Still he was not content, but explored a large extent of territory, north of Lake Erie, never before visited by a European, in what is now the Province of Ontario (Canada), beyond the point reached by him, when, for the first time, he saw the Georgian bay.

When we add to Brulé's wanderings the startling account of his barbarous murder by the Huron Indians — being not only killed but eaten by them — the story of his life forms, if not one of the strangest, at least one of the most romantic chapters of adventures wherein is related the captivity and suffering of an explorer at the hands of savages.

At almost every step in our investigations we have been surprised at the sudden appearance of events before wholly unknown to general history. This has caused as thorough an examination of incidents of apparently little interest as of those which at once impressed us with their importance. The result has been, in several instances, the establishing of facts of great consequence where, in the beginning, the clue was exceedingly dim and shadowy.

That originality is claimed for our narrative will not, it is believed, appear out of place, when it is considered that Brulé has not heretofore, except in one instance, been credited with being the first to reach any of the countries, lakes, or rivers, of which (as it is hereafter stated) he was the real discoverer or explorer.

One principal reason why the visits of Brulé to various unexplored regions have hitherto found so few historians even to refer to any of them in the most casual way is because of the exceedingly brief mention, usually, of his wanderings by early writers who have given any place in their works concerning him; and for the further reason that, when spoken of at all by the latter, it is only incidentally, and usually with such vagueness as is well calculated to repel rather than attract attention. It is not a matter of wonder, therefore, that the three or four authors of our own times who have recorded anything of his doings have expressed themselves not only with much brevity, but with unusual caution.

I desire to express my acknowledgments for favors extended while this work has been in progress to Mr. Benjamin Sulte, of Ottawa, and Very Rev. W. R. Harris, Dean of St. Catharines, Canada; Dr. Wm. H. Egle, Librarian of the Pennsylvania State Library; and Lucy M. Gay, of the University of Wisconsin.

C. W. BUTTERFIELD.

SOUTH OMAHA, NEB.,
1897.

CONTENTS.

CHAPTER I:

    Early Voyages and Discoveries in New France.—1524–1610   1

CHAPTER II:

    Stephen Brulé Arrives in New France with Champlain   12
    The Latter Goes Against the Iroquois . .   14
    Brulé Sent to the Country of the Hurons   15
    His Return to the St. Lawrence   19
    His Discoveries While Absent   20
    Acts as Interpreter, on His Return, for Champlain and the Hurons   22
    Was the First White Man to Descend the Lachine Rapids   24
    Champlain's Policy of Training Young Men as Interpreters   24
    Journey of Champlain up the Ottawa, in 1613   27
    His Failure to Discover the North Sea . .   27
    Brulé Probably Spends the Winter of 1613-'14 Among Algonquins . . .   28

CHAPTER III:

    Brulé, Accompanying Champlain, Again Starts for the Huron Country . . .   31
    He Goes as Interpreter for Champlain .   31

	PAGE
His Arrival Among the Hurons	34
Champlain Starts with Several Hundred of these Indians Against the Iroquois	35
Some Accounts of the Mohawks, Oneidas, Onondagas, Cayugas, and Senecas	36

CHAPTER IV:

Aid Offered to the Hurons by the Carantouannais from the Upper Susquehanna ... 40
Champlain, with Hurons and Algonquins, Reaches an Onondaga Stronghold and Invests it ... 46

CHAPTER V:

Brulé, with Twelve Hurons, Goes to the Carantouannais ... 47
Champlain's Attack on the Onondaga Village and its Failure ... 56
Return of the Assailants ... 58
March of the Carantouannais, with Brulé, to Assist the Hurons ... 63
Their Return to Carantouan ... 63

CHAPTER VI:

Brulé Explores the Susquehanna and Chesapeake Country to the Ocean ... 65

CHAPTER VII:

Return of Brulé to the St. Lawrence ... 87
His Remarkable Escape from Torture ... 91

CHAPTER VIII:

Brulé Discovers Lake Superior ... 107

	PAGE.
He Visits the Neutral Nation	111
Returns to Quebec	112
The Hundred Associates	114
Capture of Quebec by the English	118
Last Journey of Brulé to the Hurons	119

CHAPTER IX:

Brulé Killed and Eaten by Hurons	120
His Death Soon Known Abroad	121
The Fear of the Savages Because of Their Deed	123

APPENDIX:

NOTE I.—Champlain's Works	125
NOTE II.—Of the Hurons, Algonquins, Montagnais and Iroquois	126
NOTE III.—Exchange of Hostages—Brulé and Savignon	128
NOTE IV.—As to Brulé Being the First White Person to "Shoot" Lachine Rapids	131
NOTE V.—Signification of the Word "Carantouannais"	132
NOTE VI.—The Chouontouaroüon Identical with the Senecas	132
NOTE VII.—March of Champlain and His Hurons to the Onondaga Village.—Conflicting Views as to the Site of the Enemy's Stronghold	133
NOTE VIII.—Early Mention of the Falls of Niagara	137
NOTE IX.—Brulé's Discovery of Lakes Huron and Ontario	138

	PAGE
NOTE X.— Early Reports of Lake Erie.	141
NOTE XI.— The Home of the Eries	141
NOTE XII.— Grand Detour from the Huron Country to the Susquehanna	142
NOTE XIII.— Capt. John Smith's Discovery of the Susquehanna.— Did He Reach Pennsylvania?	144
NOTE XIV.— Concerning Brulé's Exploration of the Susquehanna River and Chesapeake Bay	147
NOTE XV.— Southern and Western Iroquois	147
NOTE XVI.— As to Brulé's Arrival at Three Rivers in 1618 and His Interview There with Champlain	150
NOTE XVII.— As to the Reliability of Brulé's Narrative	151
NOTE XVIII.— Concerning Brulé's Discovery of Lake Superior	154
NOTE XIX.— The Neutral Nation	163
NOTE XX.— As to Brulé Going Over to the English	165
NOTE XXI.— Cannibalism Among the Hurons	166
NOTE XXII.— Extracts from Sagard's "Histoire du Canada" (Paris Edition, 1866) Relating to Brulé	167
INDEX	175

ILLUSTRATIONS.

PAGE.

Iroquois Fort captured June 19, 1610 . *Frontispiece*.
Quebec in 1608 . . . . *Opposite* 12
Route of Brulé to and from the Huron Country,
    1610, 1611 . . . . *Opposite* 20
Capture of Quebec by the English, 1629   "   118
Portrait and Signature of Champlain . . "   121
Section of Champlain's Large Map of 1612 "   140
Section of Champlain's Map of 1632 . . "   159

HISTORY

OF

Brulé's Discoveries and Explorations

1610-1626

CHAPTER I.

EARLY VOYAGES AND DISCOVERIES IN NEW FRANCE.
—1524-1610.

The voyage of Columbus in the year 1492 led to that on the north by John Cabot, five years later, who probably reached the coast of Labrador and that of the island of Newfoundland. A year after, his son Sebastian explored the continent from Labrador to Virginia, and possibly as far south as Florida. The visit of the elder Cabot was supplemented by one of Gaspar Cortereal in 1500, followed by that of John Verrazzano, who, in 1524, passed up the coast from about the latitude of the present Wilmington, North Carolina, to Newfoundland. To this country he gave the name of New France, which, although subsequently restricted on the sea coast, was extended to a vast region inland.

The credit of having been the first to spread a sail upon the St. Lawrence, and of obtaining such information as afterward led to a knowledge of the whole of its valley and of a great extent of territory beyond, belongs to James Cartier, a native of St. Malo — a port in the north of France. Cartier was a skillful mariner. On April 20th, in 1534, he sailed from his native place, under orders of the French admiral, for the coast of Newfoundland, intent on exploring unknown seas and countries washed by them. He took with him sixty-one persons, in two ships of sixty tons each, and in twenty days saw the large island lying between the ocean and the river he was afterward to discover. High winds had wafted him and his men to inhospitable shores, and repairs to his ships were necessary. But this was an auspicious season of the year (May); and, upon getting again ready for sea, he boldly turned north and entered the opening of the straits of Belle Isle, already a familiar region to the hardy fishermen of civilized countries.

Having sailed nearly around Newfoundland, Cartier, after making the shore of Prince Edward island, finally entered the Chaleurs bay. In the smaller Gaspe bay, he landed and took possession of the country for the King of France. He was now at the very portal of the river of Canada, but wholly ignorant of the great waterway leading to the interior of the continent. He then sailed to the north of the island of Anticosti; thence to its western end; and, in August, started for home, reaching St. Malo early in September, having made the return voyage in less than thirty days.

Within two months after Cartier's return, a new expedition was planned. Three well-furnished ships were provided by the king. In them went, besides Cartier, one hundred and ten persons,— even some of the nobility volunteered for the voyage. All were eager to cross the Atlantic. On May 19th, 1535, the squadron sailed. But Cartier had not a pleasant summer cruise. Storms raged and the ships separated. For seven weeks they buffeted the troubled ocean. Their rendezvous was the harbor of Blanc Sablon, within the straits of Belle Isle, which they finally reached; but the omens were bad. The adventurers had confidently looked for pleasant gales and a quick voyage, and these expectations had all been blasted. Now, however, after three days, the ships moved westward along the coast of Labrador, when a harbor was entered on the northern shore. The bay was called St. Lawrence,— the name being afterward extended to the gulf and the great Canadian river. Sailing on in a southwesterly course, sighting frequently what are now known as the southern shores of the Province of Quebec, they finally discovered and ascended the St. Lawrence, reaching in September a fine harbor in an island since called Orleans.

Where the River St. Lawrence ends and the gulf begins is a matter that cannot be determined with any degree of accuracy; however, it is generally said that "the sea" is entered about four hundred and forty miles below the island just mentioned. As far up as the mouth of the Saguenay, a large northern tributary, the river is twenty miles wide; then it gradually contracts, until at a short distance above the spot where the discoverer rested its shores are less than a mile apart — the contraction being spoken of, in after years, by the Indians inhabiting the region as "quebec," or "kebec," equivalent to a "restricted channel," or "a narrowing of water."

Leaving his two largest ships in the waters of the river now known as the St. Charles, Cartier, with the smallest and two open boats, having fifty men as an escort, ascended the St. Lawrence until a considerable Indian village was reached, situated on an island called Hochelaga. Standing upon the summit of a hill, on this island, and looking away up the river, the commander had fond imaginings of future glories awaiting his countrymen in colonizing this region. He called the hill "Mont Royale;" "and time, that has transferred the name to the island, is realizing his visions;" for, on that island,[1] now stands the City of Montreal.[2]

While at Hochelaga, Cartier gathered some indistinct accounts of the surrounding country, and of the Ottawa river coming down from the hills situated to the northwest.[3] He also obtained,

[1] Now called Montreal Island.

[2] Montreal is a city of the Province of Quebec, Canada, and the commercial metropolis of the Dominion. It is situated on the south side of the island of Montreal, in the St. Lawrence river (which is here about two miles wide). It is one hundred and eighty miles from Quebec; six hundred and twenty from the gulf; and four hundred and twenty from New York. The island of Montreal is thirty-two miles long and about ten miles broad at its widest part. The city occupies a low tract about two miles wide between "Mount Royal" and the river.

[3] The Ottawa river rises near latitude 48° 36' north, and longitude 80° west. It has a southeastward course until the city of Ottawa is reached, whence it flows eastward, entering the St. Lawrence about twenty-five miles above Montreal. Its length is estimated at seven hundred miles.

while on his visit up the St. Lawrence, some crude reports concerning the upper portions of that river, and of Lakes Ontario, Erie, and Huron. He was likewise informed of the existence of copper to be found in mines, in its native or metallic state, in the (then) undefined region inland, to be reached by the Saguenay, as he was told, although the country was that bordering on the north of Lake Huron and on the south of Lake Superior.

Rejoining his ships, Cartier spent the winter in a palisaded fort on the bank of the St. Charles, with his vessels moored before it. The cold was intense. Many of his men died of scurvy. Early in the spring (May 3rd) possession was taken of the country in the name of the French king, with more ceremonies and greater jubilation than at Gaspe bay; and on July 16th, 1536, the Breton mariner dropped anchor in St. Malo,— he having returned with two ships. The other had been abandoned at his winter quarters. France was disappointed. Hopes had been raised too high. Expectations had not been realized. Further explorations, therefore, were, for the time, abandoned.

Notwithstanding the failure of Cartier's second voyage, the great valley of the St. Lawrence in all its parts was not to remain very long unknown to the world. It was thought unworthy a gallant nation to abandon such an enterprise; and one more trial at exploration and colonization was determined upon. Again the bold mariner of St. Malo started for the St. Lawrence. This was on May 23rd, 1541. He took with him five ships,— he having been commissioned captain-general and pilot of the fleet; but he went, unfortunately, as subordinate, in some respects, to John Francis de la Roche, Lord of Roberval, a nobleman of Picardy, to whom the king of France had given vice-regal powers over the country now again to be visited. The object of the enterprise was declared to be discovery, settlement, and the conversion of the Indians. Cartier was the first to sail. Again he entered the St. Lawrence, but Roberval did not make his appearance.

After erecting a fortification farther up the St. Lawrence than the old one, Cartier once more ascended the river, this time with two boats, to explore the Lachine rapids (as now called). He then returned and passed the winter at his fort; and, in the spring, not having heard from Roberval, he set sail for France.[1]

De la Roche reached the St. Lawrence during the year, but after wintering there, he, too, abandoned the country, giving back his immense viceroyalty to the rightful owners.

In 1578, there were three hundred and fifty fishing vessels at Newfoundland belonging to the French, Spanish, Portuguese, and English; besides these were a number — twenty or more — of Biscayan whalers. Subsequently, the colonization of New France was again undertaken, resulting only in forty unfortunate white men being left on Sable

---

[1] See further, as to Cartier, Ramé's *Documents Inédits sur Jacques Cartier* (Paris, 1865), pp. 10-12; Harrisse's *Notes*, pp. 1-5, 11, 12; Dionne's *Nouv. France*, pp. 9-54; Faillon's *Colonie Française en Canada*, vol. I, pp. 38-55, 496-523; Winsor's *Narrative and Critical History of America*, vol. IV, pp. 56-59,—also his *Cartier to Frontenac*, pp. 23-47, and authorities there cited; Sulte's *Canadiens-Français*, vol. II; Thwaites' *Jesuit Relations and Allied Documents* (Cleveland, 1897), vol. III, pp. 292, 293.

island, off the coast of Nova Scotia, all of whom, except twelve, died miserably in that inhospitable region.

In 1599, another expedition was resolved upon. This was undertaken by Francis Gravé, called Pontgravé, a merchant of St. Malo, and Chauvin, a captain of the marine. In consideration of a monopoly of the fur trade, granted them by the king of France, these men undertook to establish a colony of five hundred persons in New France; but these five hundred dwindled to one hundred persons. At Tadoussac, at the mouth of the Saguenay, they built a cluster of wooden huts and store houses, where sixteen men were left to gather furs, who either died or were scattered among the Indians before the return of the spring of 1601. Meanwhile, Pontgravé and Chauvin returned to France. The latter made a second voyage to Tadoussac, but failed to establish a permanent settlement. During a third voyage he died, and his enterprise perished with him.

In 1603, a company of merchants of France was formed, with Amyr de Chastes at its head, for prosecuting Canadian enterprise. Both the cross and the fleur-de-lis were to be planted in New France. Pontgravé, in command of two vessels, sailed for the St. Lawrence. SAMUEL CHAMPLAIN, a Frenchman by birth, went along, commissioned to make the most exact researches and explorations in his power.[1]

---

[1] Champlain was born at Brouage, France, in 1567. He became a captain in the royal navy. Subsequently in command of a ship he sailed to the West Indies. Before his return, he visited Vera Cruz and the city of Mexico. "Returning, he made his

Pontgravé and Champlain, after Tadoussac (that was) had been reached, ascended the river in a small bark, sailed past the lofty promontory on which Quebec now stands, and proceeded onward to the island of Hochelaga; but the Indian village visited by Cartier had disappeared. In a skiff, with a few Indians, they vainly endeavored to pass the Lachine rapids, whereupon the baffled explorers returned to their ships.

From the savages, Champlain had gleaned some knowledge of ulterior regions. The natives had drawn for him rude representations of the stream above the rapids, and of its lakes,[1] at the same time giving him some information of what must have been the great cataract of Niagara. His curiosity was inflamed, and he resolved to visit at some future day the country so full of natural wonders.

During the absence of Pontgravé and Champlain, their ships had been loaded with furs; and soon the adventurers were on their way back to

way to Panama. Here, . . . his bold and active mind conceived the plan of a ship-canal across the isthmus." His arrival in the St. Lawrence in 1603 was the next event of importance in the annals of New France following the discovery of that river by Cartier nearly seventy years before.

[1] From the gulf to the foot of Lake Ontario the river is called the St. Lawrence; from this lake to the outlet of Lake Erie it is known as Niagara; from the lake last mentioned to Lake St. Clair it is distinguished as the Detroit; from this lake to Lake Huron it is named St. Clair; from Lake Huron to the foot of Lake Superior it is called St. Mary; and from the head of this last lake to its source it is known as the St. Louis. For the purposes of historical illustration, the lakes mentioned may be considered as enlargements of a single water-course,— Lake Michigan being looked upon as the widening of a tributary. The vast region drained by this great waterway forms the "valley of the St. Lawrence;" although (in a restricted sense) the term

France.[1] Champlain had accomplished the object of his mission — the making of a brief exploration of the valley of the chief river of Canada.

It was the opinion of Champlain that on the banks of the St. Lawrence was the true site of a settlement; that here a fortified post should be erected; that thence, by following up the waters of the interior region to their sources, a western course might be traced to China, the distance being estimated by him as not more than two or three hundred leagues;[2] and that the fur trade of the whole country might be secured to France by the erection of a fort at some point commanding the route.[3] These views, five years subsequent to his visit to the St. Lawrence, induced the fitting out by Sieur de Monts, successor of De Chastes, of a

---

is applicable usually to the immediate country lying between the outlet of Lake Ontario and the head of the gulf, through which region flows the St. Lawrence.

[1] Champlain made, in all, ten voyages from France to the St. Lawrence and return; the eleventh having been terminated in Canada by his death. The times of his arrival out and of his departure were,—

Arrived 1603, May 24, departed 1603, July 11.
" 1608, June 3, " 1609, Sept. 1.
" 1610, April 26, " 1610, Aug. 13.
" 1611, May 13, " 1611, July 20.
" 1613, April 29, " 1613, July 8.
" 1615, May 25, " 1616, Aug. 3.
" 1617, June 14, " 1617, ———.
" 1618, June 24, " 1618, July 26.
" 1620, July 7, " 1624, Aug. 15.
" 1626, July 5, " 1629, Sept. (?)
" 1633, May 22 (died 1635, Dec. 25th).

[2] A league of Champlain was two and $\frac{56}{100}$ English miles.

[3] Champlain's opinions may be found fully set forth in the first of his publications relating to New France. Concerning his printed works, see Appendix to our Narrative, Note I.

second expedition, for trade, exploration, and colonization. On April 13th, 1608, Champlain, who had been made lieutenant-governor, and who was to hold the country and develop its geography, again sailed — this time with men, arms, and stores for a colony. The fur trade was entrusted to Pontgravé.

The mouth of the Saguenay was reached in June; and soon after a settlement was commenced on the brink of the St. Lawrence — the site of the present market-place of the lower town of Quebec. A rigorous winter and great suffering followed. Supplies arrived in the spring, and Champlain determined to enter upon his long-meditated explorations; — the only obstacles in the way being savage nations he would everywhere meet. He would be compelled to resort to diplomacy, — to unite a friendly tribe to his interests, and, thus strengthened, to conquer, by force of arms, the hostile one.

The Hurons, who lived near the lake which now bears their name, and their allies, the Algonquins, from the Ottawa country, also the Montagnais, dwelling upon the St. Lawrence, and to the northward, were at war, as Champlain learned, with the Iroquois — as named by the French, or (as afterward called by the English) the Five Nations — whose homes were within the present State of New York.[1] In June, 1609, he advanced, with sixty Indians of the three allied nations first mentioned and two white men, up what is now known as the Richelieu, or Sorel river,[2] to the discovery

[1] See, further, as to the Hurons, Algonquins, Montagnais, and Iroquois, Appendix, Note II.

[2] This river is also known by several other names.

of the first of the great lakes — the one which now bears his name. Upon its placid waters this courageous band was stopped by a war-party of Iroquois. On shore, the contending forces met, when a few discharges of an arquebuse sent the advancing enemy in wild dismay back into the forest. The victory was complete. Promptly Champlain returned to the St. Lawrence, and his Huron, Algonquin and Montagnais allies to their homes; not, however, until these Indians had invited him to visit their towns and aid them again in their wars. Champlain then revisited France, but the year 1610 found him once more on the St. Lawrence, determined he would never cease his explorations until he had penetrated to the western sea, or to that of the north, so as to open the way to China. But in these undertakings, to make them effective, he must have, as he had already conjectured, the help of friendly Indians. Could he command this aid? We shall now see; and we shall also discover that a white person — French like himself — was to prove an important support in his work, although a mere boy when first called to his assistance.

CHAPTER II.

STEPHEN BRULÉ ARRIVES IN NEW FRANCE WITH CHAMPLAIN.—THE LATTER GOES AGAINST THE IROQUOIS.—BRULÉ SENT TO THE COUNTRY OF THE HURONS.—HIS RETURN TO THE ST. LAWRENCE.—HIS DISCOVERIES WHILE ABSENT.—ACTS AS INTERPRETER, ON HIS RETURN, FOR CHAMPLAIN AND THE HURONS.—WAS THE FIRST WHITE MAN TO DESCEND THE LACHINE RAPIDS.—CHAMPLAIN'S POLICY OF TRAINING YOUNG MEN AS INTERPRETERS.—JOURNEY OF CHAMPLAIN UP THE OTTAWA, IN 1613.—HIS FAILURE TO DISCOVER THE NORTH SEA.—BRULÉ PROBABLY SPENDS THE WINTER OF 1613–14 AMONG ALGONQUINS.

STEPHEN BRULÉ[1] was born in Champigny, France, about the year 1592. Of his parents and his childhood, nothing is known. He came to New France in the ship commanded by Champlain, which left Honfleur on April 13th, 1608, with men, arms and stores for the settlement to be founded upon the River St. Lawrence. Above the Island of Orleans, where the stream narrows to less than a mile, a point was selected; and here, during the summer, Quebec sprang into existence, with Brulé, the subject of our narrative, as one

---

[1] Francis Parkman *(Pioneers of France in the New World,* p. 379*n*) suggests that Brulé's name "may possibly allude to the fiery ordeal through which he had passed;" that is to say, he was called "Brulé" only at a later date, after he had suffered severely at the hands of savages. While this is barely possible, it is not at all probable. The name is pronounced *bru-lay*.

ABITATION DE QVEBECQ

QUEBEC IN 1608.
(Drawn by Champlain.)

of its original inhabitants. He was one of eight persons who escaped the attacks of a scorbutic disease, which proved fatal to the other twenty who wintered at Quebec during that year

We left Champlain, the lieutenant-governor of New France, on the St. Lawrence, he having returned, in the year last mentioned, from his native country — France. He had ample power given him by his superiors either to go to war against savages or to explore unknown regions. He would do both. The Montagnais — Indians of Algonquin lineage, who occupied the surrounding wilds — had agreed to guide him toward the north, to the waters of Hudson bay, while the Hurons were to show him their great lakes and other natural wonders. As a reward for all this, he would join them aganist their common enemy — the Iroquois. But the exploration to Hudson bay was postponed for a year; nevertheless, there would be a meeting of Montagnais, Algonquins and Hurons with Champlain, as had been agreed upon, to be held at the mouth of the River Richelieu, when matters of grave import could be talked over and more definite arrangements made.

To an island[1] off the mouth of the Richelieu, Champlain repaired, taking with him his servant, the "young lad" Brulé. There, also, congregated Montagnais, but as yet no Algonquins or Hurons appeared. Suddenly, however, a canoe arrived with the startling information that the Algonquins were engaged with a hundred Iroquois who had barricaded a small spot of ground and were making a desperate defense. The Montagnais

[1] Now known as St. Ignace.

and Champlain (probably accompanied by Brulé), with four other Frenchmen, hastened to the help of their allies. Guided by the advice and skill of Champlain, the attacking savages soon gained a complete victory — other Frenchmen meanwhile having reached the scene of conflict. Fifteen Iroquois were made prisoners; the residue were either killed or drowned in the river. One of the captured was saved by Champlain; all the rest were doomed sooner or later to be tortured. One was, after death had relieved him of his suffering, quartered and eaten. The next day the Hurons appeared. There were wild orgies on the island and on the shore, as may be presumed.[1]

Preparations were soon made by the exultant savages for returning to their homes; but Champlain could not go with those who were to journey, on their way back, up the Ottawa — the reason of which does not exactly appear; doubtless, however, there were pressing reasons; but the Indians had the splendid victory over the one hundred Iroquois to console them, though probably greatly disappointed in not having the pleasure of the Frenchman's presence on their return. But Champlain was to have a substitute;— strange enough, it was to be the "young boy," Brulé, who seems to have been seized with a desire to go with the savages and acquire the language of at least some one of the nations.

There was now with Champlain, Pontgravé, the merchant of St. Malo. He had come to the St.

---

[1] For an engraving, from a drawing by Champlain, illustrating the capturing, on June 19th, 1610, of the Iroquois fort, see his *Voyages* of 1613.

Lawrence (sent by De Monts, who had a brief monopoly of the fur trade in that river), in command of a ship laden with goods for traffic with the Indians, and had sailed but a short time before Champlain started from France. Both these Frenchmen concluded that, if Brulé was really desirous of going with the savages, it would be well to consent to it. They also made up their minds to send him to the country of the Hurons, that he might ascertain the nature of that region; see their lake (then nameless, but now called Lake Huron); observe the various tribes who dwelt there; and see other objects of especial interest;[1] so that, upon his return, the facts could be better understood concerning all these things. It was with great pleasure the boy heard their resolve.[2]

An Algonquin chief present, whose name was Iroquet, had formed a very warm attachment for the Frenchman. He was asked by the latter if he would like to take the "young boy" (Champlain never once mentions Brulé's name) to his country to spend the winter with him, and to bring him back in the spring. The Algonquin chief readily

[1] "I had promised," says Champlain, previously, "the Algonquins and Ochateguins [Hurons] that I would help them in their wars, they having agreed to show me their country, the great lake [Huron], some copper mines, and other things which they had spoken to me about." This clearly indicates that they knew of the Lake Superior copper mines; for these Indians had no idea of copper except in its pure or crude state; and it was to be found in that condition in no other mines, in all the region of the Great Lakes.

[2] "I had," says Champlain, "a young lad who had already spent two winters [1609, 1610] at Quebec, and who desired to go with the Algonquins [and Hurons] to learn their language. I thought it well to send him in that direction because he could

assented to this; indeed, he seemed greatly pleased with the idea,— promising he would treat the boy as his own son. However, when Iroquet came to lay the plan before the assembled Algonquins, they were not pleased with it. They were afraid some accident might happen to the boy, in which case Champlain might be provoked to make war upon them. The enthusiasm of Iroquet was cooled by this suggestion of the Indians. The chief hastened to his white friend, telling him his companions were of the opinion that the idea was not a good one.

But Champlain had now determined to carry out the plan, if possible, and he called all the savage chiefs in council. They readily presented themselves, with others of their companions who, because of their age, or other qualifications, were relied upon as safe counsellors. "Why," said Champlain, "does Iroquet, whom I look upon as my friend, refuse to take my boy with him? This, surely, is not acting as though he held me in esteem, when he refuses to carry out what he has promised and what could only result in good to

see the country, also the great lake [Lake Huron], observe the rivers, the people, the mines [of which he (Champlain) had heard from the Hurons] and other rare things, so as to report truth about all this. He accepted the duty with pleasure." Champlain, in 1618, says Brulé had been, at that date, eight years amongst the Indians of Upper Canada; and as he was the only one of Champlain's interpreters who had seen that length of service, it is sufficiently certain that Brulé was the young man, or lad, sent, in 1610, to the Algonquins and Hurons. (Compare Laverdière's *Champlain*, pp. 368, 621.) Mr. Benjamin Sulte, in his "Annals of Ottawa," published in the Ottawa *Evening Journal*, January 12, 1889, has no doubt the "young man" (or "young lad," as Champlain terms him) of 1610, and Brulé, the interpreter, of 1618, were one and the same person.

his people. If he takes the boy, it would be the means of making us closer friends with each other and with their neighbors. But your hesitation gives me an unfavorable opinion of you. If you will not take the lad as Iroquet has promised, I will never have any more friendship for you; for you are not children, to break your promises in this manner."

This was bold language, but it was needed; and the savages were not slow to explain away their scruples. They said they were satisfied with the arrangement, only that they feared some harm might befall the boy from a change of diet — from good victuals to what was worse than he had been accustomed to; and that as a consequence the wrath of Champlain might be provoked against them. But the latter replied that the lad would be able to adapt himself to their manner of living with little or no difficulty;— he would soon become accustomed to their usual food; and should sickness or war cause him harm, it would be no cause for complaint towards them; besides, all were liable to accidents, and if any should happen to him, there must and would be on his part a proper submission to the inevitable. "Should you treat him badly or should misfortune happen to him," continued Champlain, "through your fault, I should in truth be displeased; this, however, I do not expect from you, but quite the contrary."

"Since, then," replied the chiefs, "it is your request, we will take the lad with us and treat him as one of us; but we ask you to take one of our young men in his place to go with you to France. It will be pleasant for us to hear from him upon his return about the many fine things he has seen."

Champlain accepted with pleasure the proposition made by the savages. He took the young man, a Huron, who seemed glad to go with him. He was given the name of Savignon. It was, indeed, a master-stroke of policy on the part of the Indians, and could only redound to the benefit of both sides, as it would be an additional motive with each to treat the one intrusted to them better than they otherwise might do.

Champlain fitted out young Brulé as best he could with whatever he needed, and handed him over to the care of his savage friends. Mutual promises were made to meet again at the end of the next June, when the white boy and Savignon were to be exchanged.[1] Then there was a final parting, with many promises of friendship.[2]

Champlain, on August 8th, set sail from Quebec for France. He "arrived at Honfleur with no worse accident than that of running over a sleeping whale near the Grand Bank." But he did not remain long in his native country. Before the first half of May, 1611, had gone by, he was again in Tadoussac. He was now possessed of one paramount idea — to establish such a trade with the Indian nations in circumjacent regions as would inure to the advantage of De Monts and his associates. Moving up the St. Lawrence to

[1] Appendix, Note III.

[2] Ibid. "The object of Champlain in enlisting Brulé, Nicolet, Marsolet, Hertel, Marguerie, and other grown-up boys for service in Canada, from 1608 to 1620, was to educate them as interpreters. They all could read and write; some of them were even perfect scholars."— Benjamin Sulte: "Annals of the Ottawa," in the Ottawa *Evening Journal*, Jan. 12, 1889.

the site of the present city of Montreal, he there commenced to survey the ground for a permanent trading-post. Many boats followed him up the river as eager as himself — indeed, far more so — to traffic with the Indians. Champlain modestly declares that, on May 17th, he started for "the great fall"— Lachine rapids — to meet the savages who the year previous had promised to go there with his servant [Brulé], whom he had sent with them, that he might learn from him what he had seen during the winter. In his company was the hostage, Savignon, who had returned with him from France; and he was now ready for an exchange — giving his Huron for Brulé, upon the arrival of the latter at the rendezvous previously agreed upon.

Finally, on June 13th, there appeared two hundred Hurons; also three chiefs — Ochateguin, Iroquet, and Tregouaroti, the latter a brother of Savignon. They had brought back "my servant," as Champlain expresses it. "I went to see them in a canoe with our savage,"[1] are his further words. Then there was great rejoicing. The Indians greeted Savignon. They had heard through the Algonquins (who got the report from the Montagnais) that he was dead. When they saw him before them in good health, there can be no wonder that their joy was unbounded. He spoke highly of the treatment he had received while absent, and recounted to his brother and friends many particulars concerning the remarkable things he had seen, — at which all were filled with astonishment. "I saw also my

[1] That is, with Savignon.

servant," are the unimpassioned words of Champlain, "who was dressed in the costume of the savages." Brulé was not slow to communicate to his master the fact of his having been treated with uniform kindness by the Hurons; then, too, he gave him a lengthy account of all he had seen and heard during his absence. It must have been gratifying to Champlain to discover that "the boy" had learned the Huron "language very well"—an accomplishment which was quickly utilized by his master.[1]

In going to the Huron country, Brulé was the first of Europeans to ascend the Ottawa—the first white person to stand upon the shores of Lake Nipissing—the first to descend the French river—and the first to discover Lake Huron,[2] although, of course, Champlain knew already of the existence, from Indian reports, of both these lakes and of the river last mentioned; and, of Lake Huron, Cartier had heard in 1535, although the savages reported it (as the Frenchman understood it) to be a sea.[3] The young man's arrival among

---

[1] In Champlain's recital of the sending of Brulé with the savages and of the particular events transpiring up to the time of his being first seen upon his return, the fact that he had been among the Hurons in their country is not expressly declared. Presently, however, as we follow his narrative, such will very conclusively appear. Mr. Francis Parkman, in *Pioneers of France in the New World*, p. 335n, speaks of "a youth [Brulé, as assumed in our narrative] who had volunteered the previous summer [that is, in the summer of 1610] *to go with the Hurons to their country* [the italicising is mine] and winter among them,—a proposal to which Champlain gladly assented."

[2] See Appendix, Note IX. What Brulé saw was that part of Lake Huron now known as the Georgian bay.

[3] Lescarbot's *Histoire de la Nouvelle France*, p. 381.

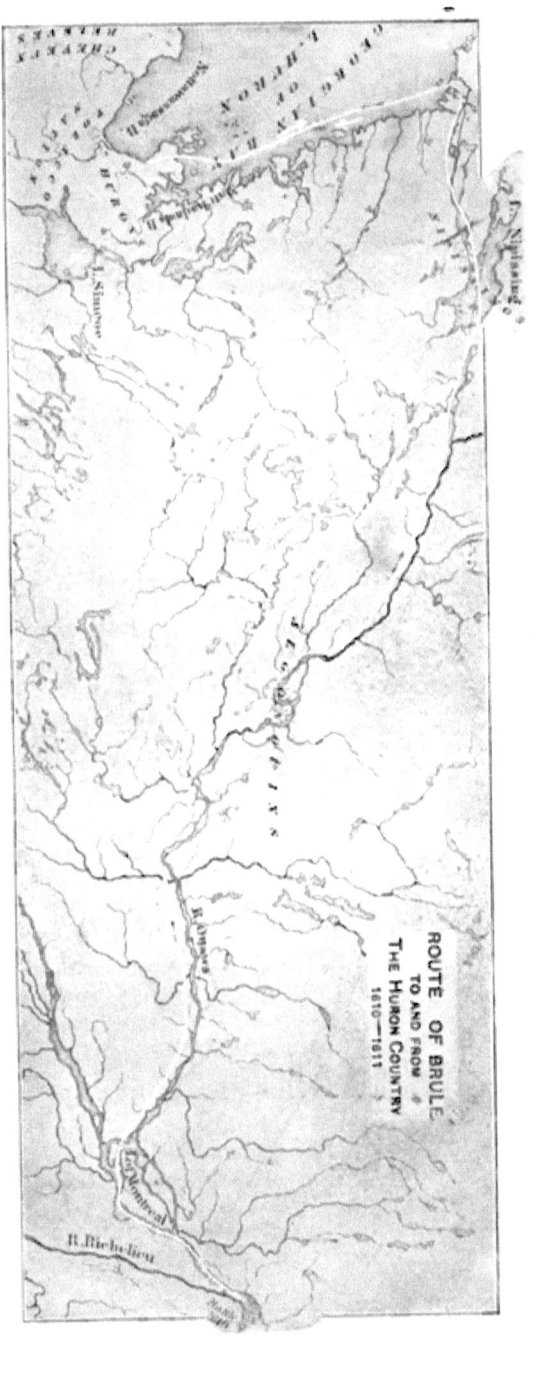

the Hurons was a source of great wonder, as but a few had ever before seen a "pale face." Champlain's "young boy" was a close observer, and in acquiring Indian languages was exceedingly ready. It was not many years before Champlain himself, with Brulé by his side, had an opportunity to test the correctness of his descriptions and conclusions of this, the first exploration ever made of the Province of Ontario.[1]

It is interesting to note the incidents occurring upon the St. Lawrence at the meeting between Champlain and the Hurons after the exchange of Brulé for Savignon, especially as to the part taken by the "young lad," now that he was, for the first time in his life, doing duty as interpreter, as will now be seen, between his countrymen and the Indians — but at this time restricted to helping Champlain on the one side and the Hurons on the other.

The number of fur-traders present excited the alarm of the Hurons. The savages gave information through Brulé that four hundred more of their people had proposed coming, but had been deterred by a report that he (Champlain) had returned to meet the Algonquins[2] with six hun-

[1] "Both of these hostages [Brulé (as we assume) and Savignon], after a mutual restitution was made the next year, became of manifest value to Champlain in his later intercourse with the savages, for this interchange of interpreters enabled him to reach better conclusions as to the great lakes of the west, and as to the passage towards Florida on the south."—Winsor, in *Cartier to Frontenac*, p. 100. It is clearly evident from Champlain's instructions to Brulé that, much as he desired his "lad" to qualify himself as interpreter, it was still more his wish he should observe closely all that was to be seen of the country and of the people who inhabited it.

[2] That is, Algonquins and Hurons.

dred Iroquois and kill them all. However, the story was not believed by those who had made their appearance. "If," said they, "we had put confidence in what we heard, we should not have come to meet you as agreed upon; but others of our people were afraid, they never having seen a Frenchman, except your servant."¹ Then the Hurons gave the further information that three hundred Algonquins would arrive in five or six days to unite with them in an expedition against the Iroquois, providing Champlain would go with them. "I talked," says Champlain, "a great deal with them about the source of the great river [St. Lawrence] and their country, and they gave me detailed information about their rivers, falls, lakes and lands, as also about the tribes living there and what is to be found in that region. . . . They told me also that, the winter before, some savages had come from the direction of Florida, beyond the country of the Iroquois, who lived near our ocean, and were in alliance with these [Huron] savages."²

Two days after the arrival of the Hurons, they became alarmed again at the appearance of so many white traders. Champlain was called, and with the aid of his "servant Brulé," and the "savage Savignon," was, during the night, successful, as he supposed, in quieting their fears. On the seventeenth, under pretense of going to

[1] As it was Hurons that were talking, this declaration of theirs makes it certain that Brulé went to their country.

[2] These savage allies of the Hurons were, as will hereafter appear, Carantouanais, or Carantouans, as named by Champlain, but more properly, Carantouannais: they were Andastes of later writers.

hunt beaver, they removed above Lachine rapids to be sure that they would be beyond the reach of the French barges, at the same time leaving Savignon with Champlain to avoid suspicion. The next day the latter was requested to go to their camp, and was told that he would soon be sent for, but to take with him only Brulé; then it was that Savignon took final leave of Champlain, who was very glad to be relieved of caring for him. He was given some trinkets and was much pleased, at the same time he feelingly mentioned that he was about to enter upon an irksome life, compared with what he had led in France.

Afterwards, Champlain was conducted, along with Brulé, to the Lake of Two Mountains, where the Hurons were encamped. It seems the Indians had heard before starting that they were all to be killed; hence their ruse in getting above the rapids. Again Champlain quieted their fears. Thereupon arrangements were made for the sending with them, on their return, a young man belonging to one of the traders. Afterwards, it was determined that one of Champlain's young men, also, should go — the latter to the Huron country for a winter's sojourn;[1] however, the other was to go only to the Algonquins, being cared for by the chief Iroquet, " who lived eighty leagues from the

---

[1] "One of our young men," says Champlain, "also determined to go with these savages, who are Charioquois [Hurons], living at a distance of some one hundred and fifty leagues from the fall [of St. Louis — Lachine rapids]. He went with the brother of Savignon, one of the captains [Tregouaroti], who promised me to show him all that could be seen." (See vol. III, p. 30, of Champlain's *Voyages — Prince Society Publications;* also Appendix to our Narrative, Note IX.)

fall"—that is, from Lachine rapids.[1] In returning to the island where was the original meeting, both Champlain and Brulé, by the aid of the savages who took them back, descended the river in safety,—Brulé, on his return from the Huron country, having been the first white person to "shoot" the falls.[2] Then the Hurons all started for their homes, the two young Frenchmen going along delighted with the prospects of enjoying a winter among the savages.

It was the middle of July before all the Algonquins reached the rendezvous. After an interchange of views and the sending with them, by Champlain, a young man whose name was Nicholas Vignau,[3] the meeting broke up; the Indians going their way and Champlain and Brulé returning to Quebec.

The policy of Champlain, begun with Brulé, was now fully developed of sending young men among the savages "to make," as he subsequently declared, "the acquaintance of the people, to learn their mode of living, and the character and extent of their territory." In other words, "to

[1] It is probable that this young Frenchman was Thomas, who afterward acted as interpreter for Champlain in going up the Ottawa in 1613, mention of which journey will soon be made.

[2] Appendix, Note IV. "The first white man to descend the rapids of St. Louis was a youth [Brulé] who had volunteered, the previous summer [that is, the summer of 1610], to go with the Hurons to their country to winter among them."—Parkman's *Pioneers*, p. 335*n*.

[3] As just explained, the young man belonging to one of the traders, and sent to the Algonquins, was cared for by Iroquet; and, as the home of that chief was farther up the Ottawa than Champlain says was reached by Vignau, the latter must have been the one sent out last.

place competent young men with the different tribes of savages, to obtain that kind of information which could only come from an actual and prolonged residence with them. This enabled him to secure not only the most accurate knowledge of their domestic habits and customs, the character and spirit of their life, but these young men by their long residence with the savages acquired a good knowledge of their language, and were able to act as interpreters. This was a matter of very great importance, as it was often necessary for Champlain to communicate with the different tribes in making treaties of friendship, in discussing questions of [importance which might arise when there was] war with their enemies, in settling disagreements among themselves, and in making arrangements with them for the yearly purchase of their peltry. It was not easy to obtain suitable persons for this important office. Those who had the intellectual qualifications, and who had any high aspirations, would not naturally incline to pass years in the stupid and degrading associations, to say nothing of the hardships and deprivations, of savage life."[1]

For the next four years — that is, from July, 1611, to the same month in 1615—history is well-nigh

[1] Rev. E. F. Slafter, in his *Historical Illustrations* of Charles Pomeroy Otis's Translations of Champlain's *Voyages* — Vol. III of the *Prince Society Publications*, p. 215*n*. Or, we might say, in the language of another, Champlain would send a number of young men to the Indians, "to have them trained to the life of the woods — to the language, manners, customs, and habits of the savages," thereby "to open through them, as advisers and interpreters, friendly relations, when the proper time should come, with the Indian nations," among whom he might travel, or "with whom he might choose to arrange a close alliance."

silent as to Brulé. All that is recorded of him is, that he lived among the savages; and it is known that meanwhile he acquired a knowledge of the language spoken by the Montagnais and by the savages of the Ottawa river and Lake Nipissing.[1] Soon after his return from the Huron country, his master (or, we might now say, his patron) again started for France. Before leaving, Champlain, it is believed, made arrangements to send once more his " boy " to live for awhile among the Indians.

After returning to Quebec, the lieutenant-governor again set his face toward France, arriving out in good time; but the next summer he was compelled to give up, for the season, all idea of going back to the St. Lawrence. It was then that Nicholas Vignau reached Paris, having spent the previous winter on the Ottawa, whither, as we have seen, he had gone the previous year. He brought accounts of what he pretended to have seen; his story was indeed " a tale of wonders." There was a great lake near the heads of the Ottawa, according to this "most impudent liar." Beyond this flowed a river to the northward. This he descended, accord-

---

[1] Sagard [*Histoire du Canada* (Paris Reprint, 1866), p. 338] afterward speaks of the trouble Brulé experienced in acquiring these languages as well as that of the Hurons: "There is another great difficulty in learning these languages [that is, the Huron, Algonquin and Montagnais], in the pronunciation of some of the syllables, which, upon being pronounced in different ways, cause the same word to have different significations. . . . This is the reason why one must study with very much difficulty the elementary sounds—and must learn the cadence if one is anxious to go ahead; for which cause, also, the interpreter Brulé has found himself sometimes very much embarrassed, and myself yet more." (See Appendix to our Narrative, Note XXII [b], where the entire extract is translated literally.)

ing to his story,—finally reaching the shores of the sea. There he had seen the wreck of an English vessel. This ocean was distant from the St. Lawrence only seventeen days by canoe. Champlain heard all this and put faith in it. The spring of 1613 found him again at Quebec, determined to go over the route pursued, as he fondly believed, by Vignau, until he had reached the North Sea. He ascended the Ottawa many a weary mile to the home of the Algonquins of Isle des Allumettes, only to discover that he had reached the point beyond which the deceiver had not journeyed. He had been duped; and, filled with indignation, he started back.

Champlain arrived at the Falls of St. Louis — Lachine rapids — on June 17th, having set out on his return on the 10th. In his company were forty canoes, increased afterwards to sixty, all belonging to Algonquins on their way to the St. Lawrence to trade with the French. After the savages had finished bartering their furs with the white traders and were on the point of returning up the Ottawa to their homes, Champlain asked them to take with them two young men,—to treat them in a friendly manner, to show them their country, and to bring them back unharmed. But the Indians objected,—at the same time calling Champlain's attention to the trouble Vignau had given him, they fearing the two who it was proposed they should take with them might bring false reports as he had done. But Champlain explained they could both be relied upon, and that, if they would not take them, he would be displeased — would look upon them all as not being his friends;

so the Indians consented to take them both along. And here it may be suggested that, possibly, one of these young Frenchmen was Brulé; indeed, in view of subsequent events, it seems quite within the range of probability that such was the fact.[1]

[1] If Brulé spent the winter of 1613-'14 among the Algonquins, he must have returned to the St. Lawrence in the summer of the year last mentioned, as early the next year his presence there is certain.

CHAPTER III.

BRULÉ, ACCOMPANYING CHAMPLAIN, AGAIN STARTS FOR THE HURON COUNTRY.—HE GOES AS INTERPRETER FOR THE LIEUTENANT-GOVERNOR.—HIS ARRIVAL AMONG THE HURONS.—CHAMPLAIN STARTS WITH SEVERAL HUNDRED OF THESE INDIANS AGAINST THE IROQUOIS.—SOME ACCOUNTS OF THE MOHAWKS, ONEIDAS, ONONDAGAS, CAYUGAS, AND SENECAS.

On the site of the present city of Montreal, there assembled, in the summer of 1615, Hurons and Algonquins, who had come down for the yearly trade with the French upon the St. Lawrence. Champlain, who had returned in May from France, was asked by the Hurons to join their bands against the Iroquois — particularly against that one of the Five Nations known afterwards to the whites as the Onondagas, living to the southward of Lake Ontario. Twenty-five hundred Indian warriors were promised to go upon the war-path. The campaign was to be on a much more comprehensive scale than anything that had preceded it, and was to be an attack on a large town situated in the heart of the present State of New York. This was distant not less than eight hundred miles by the circuitous route which it was necessary to make in reaching it. Warriors were to be collected and marshalled from the various villages of the Hurons; Algonquins also were to join them.

"The undertaking was not a small one. A journey, including the return, of fifteen hundred or two thousand miles, by river and lake, through swamps and tangled forests, with the incumbrance of necessary baggage and a motley crowd of several hundred savages to be daily fed by the chance of fishing and hunting, demanded a brave heart and a strong will. But it offered an opportunity for exploring unknown regions, which Champlain could not bring himself to decline."[1]

The lieutenant-governor, notwithstanding his previous failure to discover the "North Sea," had faith in the existence of it, and of its being located at not a great distance to the northward or northwestward of the highest point of the Ottawa reached by him in 1613. But the great unknown "sea" was Lake Superior. He had the idea, from what the savages had previously told him, that the water was salt; therefore, it must be an ocean — the same he was so anxious to discover. But first Champlain would help the Hurons and Algonquins against the Iroquois; then he would go from the country of his savage allies north until he had reached this "North Sea:" these were the two great objects he had in view; but the first was the overshadowing one.[2] However, while he was absent at Quebec making needful preparations for his journey, the Hurons became impatient and departed for their homes. With them went Father Joseph

[1] Rev. Edmund F. Slafter, A. M., in Winsor's *Narrative and Critical History of America*, vol. IV, pp. 124, 125.

[2] It was to promote the settled policy of both Champlain and Pontgravé,— the uniting of all the savage nations of New France, if possible, against the Iroquois. See, in this connection, Parkman's *Pioneers of France in the New World*, pp. 361, 362.

le Caron, accompanied by twelve armed Frenchmen. It was the intention of this missionary to learn the language of the Hurons, and labor for their spiritual welfare. His departure for his field of labor was about the first of July. On the 9th, Champlain, with two Frenchmen and ten Indians, followed him. But who were the two Frenchmen? This is, indeed (as to one of them), an important question, in its relation to our narrative. It will now be answered. One was Brulé, his trusted interpreter, who was now paid a salary of one hundred pistoles a year;[1] the other was only his waiting-man — his servant.

As we have said, the three white men, with the ten Indians as their companions, embarked on their perilous tour on July 9th, 1615. They had two canoes, which were heavily loaded and encumbered with clothes; this prevented Champlain from taking more men.[2] However, as twelve Frenchmen had already departed for the Huron country with Father Le Caron, their services would be at his command, though it was

[1] Less than two hundred dollars.

[2] "On the 9th of the month I embarked with two others, namely, one of our interpreters and my man, accompanied by ten savages in the two canoes, these being all they could carry, as they were heavily loaded and encumbered with clothes, which prevented me from taking more men."— Otis's translation of Champlain's *Voyages,*— Narrative of 1615, in the *Prince Society Publications*, vol. III, pp. 111, 112. To the word "interpreters," in the foregoing, Mr. Slafter adds a foot-note in these words: "This interpreter was undoubtedly Étienne Brûlé. It was a clearly defined policy of Champlain to send suitable young men among the savages, particularly to learn their language, and subsequently to act as interpreters. Brûlé is supposed to have been of this class."

not a very pleasant thought that only four or five of them were acquainted with the handling of fire-arms. Their journey was first by course of the Ottawa river to its junction with the Mattawan, where the former comes down from the north. Then they would follow the main stream no longer, but would turn to the left; for a northerly course would not be in the proper direction, as the Huron country was rather towards the south. So up the Mattawan they paddled their canoes, to a point where the savages were wont to land; and thence they made their way to Lake Nipissing, which they reached on the twenty-sixth of the month.

Launching their canoes upon the lake, they soon reached cabins of Nipissing Indians. They gave Champlain, with his interpreter, Brulé, and their companions, "a very welcome reception." The party tarried with them two days. The tribe numbered "from seven to eight hundred souls," who, as a general thing, lived near the lake; hence the name of that body of water. After leaving these savages, with whom he had feasted not only on fish from the lake, but on game from the forest, Champlain "entered a river, by which this lake discharges itself"— now known as French river. Finally, he reached Lake Huron — the great lake he had heard of so often — which he first speaks of as the lake of the Attigouautans, that is, the lake of the Hurons, but which, in view of its great extent, he afterward named "Mer Douce" (Fresh Sea). This portion of the lake has since received the name of Georgian bay.

After a while, as they paddled their canoes

southward, their " provisions began to give out in consequence of the bad management of the savages, who ate so heartily at the beginning that towards the end very little was left," although the party had but one meal a day. But the ten Indians proceeded to gather some squashes on shore, which Champlain says were acceptable; and they did not lack for berries; "otherwise," he declares, "we should have been in danger of being reduced to straits."

While Champlain was engaged in replenishing his larder, he suddenly came upon a band of three hundred Indians. These savages, because of the peculiar mode of arranging their hair, he called " Cheveux Relevés " — a name afterwards given by the French to the Ottawas, a kindred people. They were of a numerous tribe inhabiting the region west and southwest of Nottawassaga bay of Lake Huron. Entering into conversation with one of their chiefs, Champlain inquired in regard to the extent of their country, which the savage pictured, doubtless rudely, on the bark of a tree.[1]

Champlain's course continued southward along the eastern shore of the Georgian bay until they arrived at what is at present called Matchedash bay, across which, in a southwesterly direction, they urged their frail canoes, until the landing was reached; and they were in the country of the

[1] As the Cheveux Relevés were of Algonquin lineage, and as Brulé had acquired the language of the Algonquins of the Ottawa, Champlain could not have had much difficulty in communicating with the savage chief mentioned above, through the young Frenchman — his interpreter.

Hurons.[1] Some seventeen or eighteen miles' travel inland brought them, on the first day of August, to a Huron village called Otoüacha.[2]

Once among the Hurons, Champlain found a marked change in the country. "It was here very fine, the largest part being cleared up, and many hills and several rivers rendering the region agreeable." These localities seemed to the three white men very pleasant in comparison with the disagreeable region through which they had passed on their journey hither. Soon, three more Indian villages were visited, till at length Carhagouha, an important town of the nation, was reached. A triple palisade of wood, thirty-five feet high, served as its defence. Here, Father Le Caron was found and the twelve Frenchmen who had accompanied him. There were now, therefore, in the Huron country, sixteen white men. Mass was celebrated on August 12th by the Récollet friar.

The grand object of Champlain's visit must not be lost sight of. It was to aid the savage Hurons in an expedition against an implacable foe. But the Indians were slow in assembling. Champlain, on August 14th, with eight of Le Caron's men and his own two Frenchmen, one of whom of course was Brulé, started for Cahiagué, the chief of the Huron villages, where the warriors were to rendezvous. In three days, three Indian towns were visited; when, on the 17th,

---

[1] There were four tribes of the Huron nation — the Bear, the Wolf, the Hawk, and the Heron. The first-mentioned ("Attigouautan") was the principal one. The four were not nations forming a confederacy, as generally supposed.

[2] Synonyms: Toanché, Toanchen, Toanchain, Toachim, Teandeoniat, Otoucha.

they arrived at the point of destination. Cahiagué contained two hundred large cabins. The white men were "received with great joy and gladness by all the savages of the country," says Champlain. For when the Hurons who were upon the St. Lawrence left that river for their homes, after waiting some time for his return to them to go with them as he had promised, it was the belief of many he was dead or that the Iroquois had captured him. It was this that now caused the delay in the expedition; as the savages had postponed the undertaking for one year. However, the actual presence of the white men, though but eleven in number, caused a quick rallying of warriors — they swarmed in from every quarter.

The greater portion of the savages having assembled, Champlain set out from Cahiagué on the first day of September and passed along the shore of a small lake — Couchiching — into which flow by a small stream the waters of Lake Simcoe. Here a rest was taken until all the Hurons who were to go upon the expedition had got together, when, "shouldering their canoes and scanty baggage, the naked host set forth,"[1] accompanied by Champlain, his waiting-man (but not by his interpreter), and by eight of the Frenchmen who had journeyed to the Huron country with Le Caron. But why not by his interpreter? — Where was the intrepid Brulé? — a question soon to be answered. But what shall we say of the enemy against whom Champlain had now taken up his line of march?

---

[1] How many actually marched is unknown; but it seems altogether certain the number was much less than what had been promised Champlain.

and what of the country which they then inhabited?

The Mohawks, Oneidas, Onondagas, Cayugas and Senecas (as these nations were afterward known to the English) occupied, in 1615, the central portion of what is now the State of New York. They were the Iroquois — Five Nations — already mentioned. The Onondagas, at the time of Champlain's visit to the Hurons, were known by the latter as Entouhonorons.[1] They lived in fifteen towns built in strong situations, and along with the four other nations just mentioned were enemies of all surrounding ones (except the "Neutrals," who resided to the westward of the Iroquois), including, among these, the nations of which were the bands now on the war-path with Champlain. The country of the Onondagas is mentioned by Champlain as a fine one, with a good climate. They tilled the soil, and, with the other four nations, spoke a language radically the same as that of the Hurons. But Champlain recognized as Iroquois only the most easterly of the Five Nations; for he had no knowledge of the extent of the league — knowing only that those whom he designated as Iroquois (that is, the Mohawks) united with the Entouhonorons (Onondagas) and Senecas, in making war on surrounding nations.

[1] Whenever Champlain speaks of this nation *in the text* of any of the editions of his works he invariably calls them the Entouhonorons.

CHAPTER IV.

AID OFFERED TO THE HURONS BY THE CARANTOU-
ANNAIS FROM THE UPPER SUSQUEHANNA.—CHAM-
PLAIN, WITH HURONS AND ALGONQUINS, REACH-
ES AN ONONDAGA STRONGHOLD AND INVESTS IT.

There dwelt, at this period, three good days' journey to the southward of the Entouhonorons (Onondagas), which nation Champlain and his Hurons were on the march to attack, a nation, already mentioned, known to the latter as Carantouannais.[1] These Indians were very warlike; and, although they had but three villages, which were in the midst of more than twenty other unfriendly ones, on which they made war, they maintained their ground because of their prowess.[2] They had for their allies the Hurons. Carantouan, their principal town,[3] was sometimes visited by ambassadors

---

[1] As to the signification of the name "Carantouannais," see Appendix, Note V.

[2] The information as to the Carantouannais having "but three villages, which were in the midst of more than twenty other unfriendly ones," is from Champlain. But this needs an explanation. While the Carantouannais proper had but that many towns, friendly tribes to the southward were very numerous. From Champlain's standpoint it seemed that they were surrounded by the hostile Iroquois, who had numerous villages; whereas the latter were all to the northeast, to the northward, or northwestward; and none of these towns were probably nearer than eighty or ninety miles from the most northerly of those inhabited by the Carantouannais.

[3] In the edition of 1619 of Champlain's *Voyages*, the chief town of the Carantouannais is mentioned as Carantouan, but in the Narrative of his Expedition of 1615, given therein, the village is not spoken of.

of the nation last named, and the Carantouannais repaid the compliment by occasionally sending delegates to the homes of the Hurons. It is indeed certain that their forces had in previous years been united occasionally against the common enemy — the Iroquois. The language of the one was in many of its words either the same or similar to that of the other; both used Iroquois dialects.[1] Champlain declares the Carantouannais lived in a very fine country; and that the nation was securely quartered there, notwithstanding they were at war with the Entouhonorons (Onondagas).[2]

Now, it is evident from the distances given, that the country of the Carantouannais was upon the upper waters of the Susquehanna, and not far away from the line which now separates the State of New York from Pennsylvania. Carantouan was a palisaded town with a population of eight hundred warriors,— about four thousand souls. The dwellings and defences were like those of the Hurons.[3]

[1] Compare Prof. A. L. Guss's article entitled "Early Indian History of the Susquehanna," published in the *Historical Register*, vol. I (January, 1883), pp. 40, 43.

[2] "Carantouanis [Carantouannais]. This is a tribe that has moved to the south of the Antouhonorons [Entouhonorons] and dwells in a very fine country, where it is securely quartered. They are friends of all the other tribes, except the above named Antouhonorons, from whom they are only three days' journey distant."— *Index to Champlain's Map of* 1632 (see *Publications of the Prince Society—Champlain's "Voyages,"* vol. I, p. 304). On the map (same vol. and p.), the Entouhonorons are mentioned as Antouoronons. But, as Champlain previously explains (which fact is overlooked in the Index to the map), the Carantouannais were not friends to all the other tribes except the Entouhonorons (Onondagas).

[3] It has been suggested that the site of Carantouan was at or near that of the present Waverly, Tioga county, New York.

DISCOVERIES AND EXPLORATIONS. 39

To a just understanding of the location of the Carantouannais, and the difficulty they had to encounter in conferring with their Huron allies, it is necessary to make mention of the situation of each of the five Indian nations located to the northeastward, to the northward, and to the northwestward of them, and which were their enemies.

The most easterly of the Iroquois were the Mohawks; and it was this tribe that, in 1609, was attacked by Champlain on the western shore of the lake which bears his name. Immediately to the westward of them were the Oneidas, whose territory extended from a point below what is now Utica, Oneida county, in the present State of New York, to Deep Spring, near Manlius, Onondaga county. Then came the Onondagas, whose country reached west of the Oneidas to a line between Cross and Otter lakes. Beyond the nation last mentioned were the Cayugas, whose villages were on Cayuga lake. Still farther to the westward were the Senecas; their territory reached to the Genesee river,— these Indians being known to the Hurons in 1615 as the Chouontouaroüon;[1] and Champlain mentions that the Hurons — the allies of the Carantouannais — would have to pass through their country, or else make a very long

---

Waverly is located on Cayuta creek, which rises in Schuyler county, that State, in a small lake of its own. It runs first southeastward, drains parts of Chemung and Tioga counties, and enters the Susquehanna river in Pennsylvania two or three miles above Athens. Waverly is a post village in Barton township, Tioga county, and is eighteen miles east-southeast of Elmira, nineteen miles west-southwest of Owego, and four miles north of Athens, Bradford county, Pennsylvania.

[1] See Appendix, Note VI.

circuit ("grand detour," as Champlain expresses it), in visiting the Carantouannais.¹ The Senecas, when first visited by white people, were the most populous of the Five Nations. And Champlain declares the Chouontouaroüon were numerous.

Upon Champlain's arrival at Cahiagué and before his starting upon the war-path with his Indian allies against the Onondagas, he learned what was of great interest to him, that there was a prospect of help in their proposed expedition which was wholly unexpected. It came from the Carantouannais. It is believed these Indians had knowledge of the journeying of the Hurons to the St. Lawrence for the purpose of trade and of their intended proposal to Champlain to engage him if possible to assist them against the Onondagas; and it is certain that, being willing to aid the undertaking themselves, they had sent word to their allies informing them of their desire to help them in the campaign with a force of five hundred "good men." It is not a matter of wonder that such an offer should have been made, as the Iroquois, it was well known to the Hurons, also made war upon these their allies. It was also a part of the

¹ The Chouontouaroüon, that is, the Senecas, are described in the Jesuit *Relation* for 1648 (Quebec ed., pp. 46-48) as living between the Hurons of Canada and the Carantouannais. This corresponds with what Champlain says (see Laverdière's *Champlain*, vol. I, p. 522): "In going from one [the Hurons] to the other [the Carantouannais], a grand detour is necessary, in order to avoid the Chouontouaroüon, which is a very strong nation." (See Appendix to our narrative, Note VI; and as to this "grand detour," Note XII. This then well known and much traveled Indian route is marked on Champlain's map of 1632 by a dotted line reaching from Lake Erie — which lake is but vaguely indicated — to the Susquehanna.)

information received that the Carantouannais wished to see the French and give expression to the pleasure they would have in making their acquaintance, and to form an alliance and establish a friendship with them, that they might engage in the war together. This was particularly gratifying to Champlain, as he saw in the offer of these savages, as he hoped, an opportunity to learn something of their country.

It was not until Champlain finally gave his consent late in the previous June to the assembled Hurons upon the St. Lawrence that he would join them in an expedition against the Iroquois, that any word could have been dispatched to the Carantouannais of the fact. As the news must have gone, if at all, by way of the Huron country to them, it is certain that there was not time for such a message to have been sent them and an answer returned to Cahiagué before the seventeenth of the following August — the date of Champlain's arrival. Double the time would at least have been required. The proposition then from the Carantouannais was to assist the Hurons, whether the latter were aided by Champlain or not.

Besides their proffered aid, the Carantouannais sent information that greatly interested Champlain. He learned that Carantouan was only seven days' journey from where the Dutch ("Flamens") went to traffic with Indians, at "Fort Nassau," near the present city of Albany, New York. "The savages there," says the lieutenant-governor, "assisted by the Dutch, make war upon them [the Carantouannais], take them prisoners and cruelly put them to death."[1] This fact was not only made known to the Hurons, but they were informed also that, the preceding year (1614), the Carantouannais captured three of those white people who were assisting their enemies; and while in action one of the Carantouannais was killed. Nevertheless, they did not fail to send back the three Dutch prisoners without doing them any harm, supposing that they belonged to the whites who were assisting the Hurons, since they had no knowledge of the French except by hearsay,— they never having seen a Christian; otherwise, they said the three prisoners would not have got off so well. If others should be taken, they would not be returned to their friends.[2]

No action, as already intimated, was immediately taken by the Hurons concerning the proposition of the Carantouannais. It would be time enough when they could feel assured that the expedition would be undertaken; so, when all the bands had arrived below the outlet of Lake Simcoe, then it was that a consultation was had for the selection of a few of the warriors to carry advice to the Carantouannais of the departure of the Hu-

[1] Champlain puts the place "Fort Nassau" on the 40th parallel of latitude; but in this he was in error, he supposing the Indians who were assisted by the Dutch were of those living near Manhattan island, which he placed in that latitude (see his Map of 1632).

[2] Champlain's *Voyages* (ed. of 1619), in the Narrative of his Expedition of 1615.

In the Index to Champlain's Map of 1632, it is said that once they [the Carantouannais] took as prisoners some Flemish [Dutch], but sent them back again without doing them any harm, supposing that they were French. This is but a repetition of Champlain's declaration, mentioned above, as to the capture of three "Flamens."

rons, that they might join the latter and together attack the enemy's stronghold. The result of the deliberation was that there should be despatched two canoes, with twelve of their most robust warriors, to their allies, to inform them that their proposition was accepted, and that they would be expected at a place selected as the rendezvous, on a certain day — the eleventh of October. One of Champlain's white companions solicited the privilege of going along with the Huron party. Champlain willingly permitted him, as he would see the country of the Carantouannais by that means, and acquire a knowledge of the people who inhabited it. The danger was not trifling, inasmuch as they had to pass through the country of their enemies, the Chouontouaroüon; that is, the Senecas. The white man thus permitted to go was Champlain's own interpreter — Brulé.[1]

We now see why it was that Brulé did not accompany the few white men and the Huron warriors farther on their expedition. It gladdened the heart of Champlain, as his words clearly show, to find an opportunity for gratifying a desire of obtaining information of a region so wholly unknown to him.[2]

Let us now follow Champlain and his nine white

[1] Evidently it was that he (Champlain) believed by consenting to let his interpreter go with the twelve Hurons much might be learned of a country not before explored. This, it is clear, was his principal reason.

[2] Champlain, in his Narrative of 1618, changes his reasons given in that of 1615 for permitting Brulé to accompany the twelve Hurons to the Carantouannais; but, in so doing, it is evident his memory was at fault; finally, however, he recovers his lost ground somewhat by saying that Brulé left him *to engage in the explorations* which he (Brulé) subsequently made.

men and the savages with whom they marched (consisting mostly of Hurons, but with them were some Nipissings and Algonquins)[1] on the war-path from the outlet of Lake Simcoe to the village of the Onondagas — the objective point of the expedition.

Coasting along the northeast shore of the lake just mentioned, the savage warriors and Frenchmen, after a journey of five or six leagues, reached a point nearest to Sturgeon lake. After carrying their canoes some ten leagues, the Indians, with Champlain and his few white companions, reached the body of water last spoken of, out of which flows what is now known above Rice lake as the Otonabee river, but below as the Trent, which discharges into Lake Ontario; so that, from Sturgeon lake their course was a continuous water route to "the great lake of the Entouhonorons," as the Hurons called Lake Ontario, meaning thereby, of course, "the lake of the Onondagas."

Champlain and his dusky host had proceeded thus far by short days' journeys, constantly hunting as they progressed. At the eastern extremity of Lake Ontario, which is the entrance to the St. Lawrence, the traverse was made, — large, beautiful islands being especially noted. About fourteen leagues were made in passing to the eastern side of the lake towards the territory of the enemy. The savages now concealed all their canoes in the woods near the shore. The whole force then

[1] Champlain had already distinguished between the Indians of Lake Nipissing and those upon the Ottawa below, calling the former Nipissings and the latter Algonquins. Of the last mentioned who went with him, was the chief Iroquet already spoken of.

moved some four leagues over a sandy strand, where Champlain observed a very pleasant and beautiful country, intersected by many little streams and two small rivers, which empty into Lake Ontario; also many ponds and meadows, where there was an endless amount of game, many vines, fine woods, and a large number of chestnut trees, whose fruit was still in the burr. The chestnuts were small, he declares, but of good flavor.

After leaving the border of the lake, the Hurons and white men continued their course by land for "about twenty-five or thirty leagues." In the space of four days, many brooks were crossed, including also a river which proceeded from a lake,—its waters finally emptying into Lake Ontario. It is altogether certain that this was what is now known as Oneida river, and that the crossing was at the outlet of Oneida lake; for Champlain describes it as near a lake, which is "twenty-five or thirty leagues in circuit," and which contains some fine islands, and is the place where our enemies, the Iroquois, catch their fish, in which it abounds. Now, the Oneida is the only lake in this region containing any islands. The outlet of the lake is frequently indicated in early maps;—it was known to many early explorers as "the great fishery."

Having crossed the Oneida river, the invading savages, on October 9th, sent out a reconnoitering force,[1] which, when distant some four (French) leagues (about ten miles) from the ene-

[1] The language of Champlain as to this reconnoitering of the savages is vague. It would imply, if taken literally, that *all* of the Indians went out, leaving the Frenchmen behind. But this, certainly, would not have been done.

my's village, came upon a party of their foes, consisting of four women, three boys, one girl, and three men, who were going fishing.[1] These were, of course, easily captured. As a prelude to a general sacrifice of the prisoners, a finger of one of the squaws was cut off; but, at the earnest interference of Champlain, all were saved except the men, who were promptly tortured to death.[2] On the next day, at three o'clock in the afternoon, the whole force arrived before the Onondaga town.

The territory of the Onondagas, in 1615, was the most favorable for an invasion by the Hurons of any occupied by the Iroquois; and of this fact the latter were well advised. They were marching in such force as evidently justified an attack upon a large village of the enemy. It may, therefore, be assumed that the point aimed at was not an inferior town, but one of the strongholds of the nation. It is only known with absolute certainty that it was situated on or near some one of the lakes, ponds, or streams whose waters find an outlet into Lake Ontario through the Oswego river, and not far away, either above or below, the latitude of the present city of Syracuse, and between the longitude of the east end of the Oneida lake and that of the west side of Lake Onondaga.[3]

[1] A misapprehension by some writers of the language of Champlain concerning the "four leagues"—about ten miles—has caused much confusion in their investigations. It is not that the "great fishery" was four leagues from the objective point of the expedition, but the prisoners were captured at that distance from it. (See Appendix, Note VII.)

[2] The chief Iroquet, who, although an Algonquin, seems to have been the most prominent leader of the savages, coolly told Champlain that he would spare the women, but the men should be tortured according to their custom.

[3] See Appendix, Note VII.

CHAPTER V.

BRULÉ, WITH TWELVE HURONS, GOES TO THE CA-
RANTOUANNAIS.—CHAMPLAIN'S ATTACK ON THE
ONONDAGA VILLAGE AND ITS FAILURE.—RETURN
OF THE ASSAILANTS.—MARCH OF THE CARAN-
TOUANNAIS, WITH BRULÉ, TO ASSIST THE HU-
RONS.—THEIR RETURN TO CARANTOUAN.

It was on September 8th, 1615, that Brulé and his twelve dusky companions started for Carantouan.[1] It was the interpreter's restless spirit and ardent love of adventure that prompted him to ask permission to form one of the party. The possibility (nay, probability) of meeting savage enemies did not deter him. The prospects of suffering in any way, he did not brood over. He had that fearless nature which took no account of obstacles, however threatening they might appear. Savage life had positive pleasures

---

[1] Champlain asserts subsequently (that is, in his Narrative of 1618) that Brulé, after having taken leave of him to go on his journey and execute his commission, set out with the twelve savages whom he had given him for the purpose of showing the way and to serve as an escort on account of the dangers which he might have to encounter. But, in all this, his memory was sadly at fault.

" At this point they despatched twelve of the most stalwart savages, with the interpreter, Étienne Brûlé, on a dangerous journey to a distant tribe dwelling on the west [south] of the Five Nations, to urge them to hasten to the fort of the Iroquois, as they had already received word from them that they would join them in this campaign."—E. F. Slafter: *Memoir of Samuel de Champlain*, in *Prince Society Publications of Champlain's "Voyages,"* vol. I, p. 128.

for him, and its perils only intensified his liking for it.

It is not asserted by Champlain that Brulé was armed and equipped for his journey as were the white men who were with the Huron warriors; on the contrary, it is reasonably certain that he had nothing but the simple means of defense possessed by his savage companions. Their route was not what would lead them eastward through the small lakes and down the river Trent to the foot of Lake Ontario and across to the southeast shore of that body of water — thence through the very center of the Iroquois territory to the homes of the Carantouannais; such a course would have been far too dangerous.[1] They must, therefore, go southward, carrying their two frail bark canoes for transportation on water-courses necessary to follow or to cross, until Lake Ontario was reached. There were two streams, one from the southward emptying into Lake Simcoe, another, the Humber, from the northward flowing into Lake Ontario, which were to be their highway of travel, there being a short portage from one to the other, across which the two canoes could easily be carried. It was not a long journey to the lake and the route was well known to the Hurons. Afterwards, it was frequently traveled in going to the St. Lawrence, the journey occupying but ten days, thus avoiding the numerous obstacles of the Ottawa. Even as early as 1632 it was recorded by a French writer, who

---

[1] Parkman (*Pioneers*, p. 377) says, in a general way, that Brulé crossed Lake Ontario; but he is led to say this only by observing that the Carantouannais lived to the southeastward of it, while Brulé was then to the northwestward,— not from any authority that the latter actually paddled his canoe across the lake.

was then among the Hurons, that the latter assured him "it was only ten days' journey" by way of Lake Ontario "to the trading-place" on the St. Lawrence. Before 1670, the course along the north shore of Lake Ontario to the mouth of the Humber, thence up that river and across to Lake Simcoe, thence down the Severn to the Georgian bay, was a well-traveled one.[1]

Had Brulé journeyed along the usual land-route by way of the Neutral villages, hereafter to be mentioned, it would have taken him about ten days to have reached the Niagara river,— passing first out of the present county of Simcoe, then through what are now the counties of Dufferin, Peel, Halton, Wentworth and Lincoln. But the route he actually traveled only occupied him and his twelve savages a little over half the time which the other course would have necessitated, — going, after leaving Simcoe, through York county to the lake; thence along its shores in Peel, Halton, Wentworth and Lincoln, to the mouth of the Niagara.

That Brulé and the twelve Huron savages took their way first towards the head of Lake Ontario instead of going towards its outlet, it is evident was to save time and, in the end, not to pursue the dangerous route — one wholly impracticable, in fact,— through the heart of the Iroquois country. At the mouth of the Humber, Brulé first saw On-

[1] Writing of the year 1670, Parkman says: "The Jesuits and fur-traders, on their way to the Upper Lakes, had followed the route of the Ottawa, or, more recently, that of Toronto and the Georgian bay" (*La Salle and the Discovery of the Great West*, ed. of 1880, p. 19). And, in 1680, La Salle took the same route in going to the Illinois (Id., p. 189).

tario's broad expanse. Its existence had, as already intimated, been made known to the civilized world, but the intrepid interpreter was the first white man to reach its shores. Coasting along the lake, probably, the party soon reached the mouth of the Niagara.[1] The river, it is to be inferred, was not followed by them up to the great cataract;[2] and it is doubtful if Brulé obtained any particular knowledge of the Attiwandarons (or Neutrals),[3] or of Lake Erie;[4] neither is it likely that he visited the Eries ("Cat nation"), the homes of which were south of that body of water.[5]

After leaving the Niagara river, an easterly course must be taken to Carantouan; this would necessitate, in order to save time, leaving some outlying Neutral villages to the south, which, naturally enough, Brulé and his Hurons would not care to visit, and then proceeding onward for two or three days until the Seneca territory was reached. Now the Senecas were arch enemies of the Hurons; and a direct line from the mouth of

[1] See Appendix, Note IX.

[2] The falls are noted on Champlains map of 1632; but it seems certain the intrepid Frenchman did not see the cataract, or it would have been very differently spoken of in the Index to that map. (See Appendix to our Narrative, Note VIII.)

[3] The Neutral nation (so called because of their observing a neutral policy as to the Hurons and Iroquois) had four or five villages east of the Niagara river, one of which was only a day's journey from the home of the Senecas. (See Appendix, Note XIX.)

[4] Lake Erie would unquestionably have otherwise appeared on Champlain's map of 1632 had Brulé reached its shores. (See Appendix, Note X.)

[5] "The Eries who dwelt to the south and east of Lake Erie were called by the early French the Nation of the Cat, from the

the Niagara river to Carantouan would lead through their settlements. There was no alternative, therefore, for Brulé and his twelve Hurons, but to take a course near their villages, as they must avoid, for want of time, the wide circuit— the "grand detour"— usually made to the westward, to the southwestward, and to the south of the Seneca country.[1] In any event, they must expose themselves to danger; but to make it as little as possible, after having determined not to go far out of the way, they must pursue a less direct route than they would otherwise follow if peace existed between the Senecas and Carantouannais. Crossing the Niagara river into what is now Western New York, in the present county of Niagara, the journey was doubtless pursued through what are now the counties of Erie, Genesee, Wyoming, Livingston, Steuben and Chemung, into Tioga,— "through thick and [almost] impenetrable forests, wood and brush, marshy bogs, frightful and unfrequented places and wastes." But with all their care—in spite of all their caution — while crossing an open spot — prob-

---

large number of wild-cats or lynxes that filled their forests. The Iroquois called the Neutrals the 'Cats,' for the same reason. No mission was ever opened among this tribe [the Eries]. It is not probable that they were ever visited by a white man, unless Étienne Brulé, Champlain's interpreter, went among them in 1615."— Harris, in *Early Missions in Western Canada*, p. 242n.

That Brulé did not visit the Eries seems altogether certain for these reasons: (1) Champlain has no account of them in his *Voyages* (ed. of 1619); (2) Brulé had no time to spare in going to the Carantouannais; and (3) the Eries had only a nominal occupation of the country east of Lake Erie. Their villages were south of that lake (see Appendix to our Narrative, Note XI).

[1] See Appendix, Note XII.

ably a dried-up marsh — they "encountered some hostile savages who were returning to their villages." The enemy (Senecas) were worsted by the white man and his Hurons — four were killed and two made prisoners. The last-mentioned were taken along by Brulé and his companions — all soon after reaching Carantouan.[1]

Brulé, then, was the first of civilized men to traverse that part of the country. No white man had preceded him in that region. To him, therefore, is due the credit of having been its first explorer, — the first to set foot upon any portion of the present State of New York west of the upper part of the East Branch of the Susquehanna. And the date of his journey was 1615 — a little over eight years only after the settlement of Jamestown and six after the first white man ascended the Hudson.

But the arrival of Brulé could not have awakened in the minds of the four thousand men,

[1] "One of his [Champlain's] men, Stephen Brulé, started with twelve Indians to communicate their plans to their allies, the Carantouannais, and reached their town after daringly crossing the enemy's country."—John Gilmary Shea, in *The Pennsylvania Magazine of History and Biography*, vol. II, p. 105.

"On the first of September, 1615, the Huron warriors left Lake Couchiching and proceeded to Lake Simcoe, where they made a halt. From that place, Brulé took leave of Champlain after receiving his instructions, and traveled in the direction of Lake Erie. . . . He and his twelve Indians passed 'through the enemy's territory,' which means in few words, that they went from Lake Simcoe straight to [towards] Buffalo, [to] the country inhabited by the . . . . Senecas, the most southerly [westerly] tribe of the Iroquois. There they saw 'a few of the enemy returning to their village' and without any more ado killed four and took two of them prisoners of war."— Benj. Sulte, in *The Evening Journal*, Ottawa, Canada, Oct. 29th, 1892.

women and children of Carantouan that profound astonishment which the sight of a white man might be expected to have produced; as already Dutch prisoners had been taken to their village, as before explained.

The Hurons and Frenchman were welcomed with great joy by the Carantouannais,— the strangers being entertained with banquets and dances, in a manner to gladden the hearts of their guests after such a long and difficult journey. The rejoicing continued for some days.

The Carantouannais now assembled in their village in council to deliberate and resolve in regard to sending the five hundred warriors to the assistance of their Huron allies, who, they had been assured, would soon invest the stronghold of the Onondagas, helped on by Champlain and other white men.[1] The result of the conference was to adhere to their original offer of help. Orders were therefore given to collect, prepare and arm their warriors and that the latter should march to the aid of their allies to meet them at the place suggested by the Hurons, at their council near Lake Simcoe, which place was only three short days' journey from Carantouan.[2] But the five hundred

[1] It is declared by Champlain in his Narrative of 1618 that after Brulé had told them (the Carantouannais) his mission and explained to them the occasion of his journey, the savages of the place assembled in council to deliberate and resolve in regard to sending the five hundred warriors *asked for by Brulé*. But this is giving altogether too much authority to Brulé. So far as the five hundred men were concerned,— it was his mission only to aid the twelve Hurons in hurrying them up.

[2] Champlain's *Voyages*, ed. of 1619: Narrative of his Expedition of 1618. Champlain's assertion that Carantouan was a *short* three days' journey from the Onondaga village was in accordance

"were very long in getting ready, although urged by Brulé to make haste, who explained to them that if they delayed any longer they would not find" their allies at the rendezvous fixed upon by them. Finally, about October 15th, with Brulé accompanying them, they set off,— with what success the sequel will show.

It was, it will be remembered, three o'clock in the afternoon of October 10th, 1615, that Champlain, with his Indians and nine white men, reached and invested the Onondaga stronghold — the objective point of their expedition. "The village was enclosed by four good palisades, which were made of great pieces of wood, interlaced with each other, with an opening of not more than half a foot between two, and which were thirty feet high, with galleries after the manner of a parapet, which they had furnished with double pieces of wood that were proof against . . . . . arquebus shots. Moreover, it was near a pond where the water was abundant, and was well supplied with gutters, placed between each pair of palisades, to throw out water, which they had also under cover inside, in order to extinguish fire."

Immediately skirmishing was indulged in between the contending savages. It was Champlain's desire that the presence of white men with fire-arms should not be disclosed to the enemy until

with information furnished him by Brulé some time after the latter visited the Carantouannais. This does not necessarily conflict with Champlain's statement in his Narrative of 1615, that the Carantouannais were a *good* three days' journey from the Onondagas, as will hereafter be explained.

the next day; however, impatience on the part of
the Hurons and their anxiety to rescue some of
their warriors who were hotly pursued made it
incumbent on the part of the "pale faces" not
only to show themselves at once, but to open fire
with their arquebuses. Speedily the Onondagas
fled inside their stockade, carrying with them their
dead and wounded; and the besiegers also withdrew
to their main body with five or six wounded,
one of whom died.[1]

Champlain was far from being pleased at this
weak attempt of his Huron allies. Angry words
were showered upon them by the excited Frenchman.
Then he proceeded, after his admonition,
to instruct them in the art of war. He would have
their camp fortified to some extent. He would
have a wooden tower made with a sufficient hight
to overlook the stockade of the enemy, and large
enough to give protection to four or five marksmen.
His savage allies quickly comprehended his
scheme, which included also the making of movable
parapets to serve as shields from the arrows
and stones of the besieged. The next day, in the
early hours, aided doubtlessly by the Frenchmen
who were with them, the savages set to work upon
the tower and parapets and in less than four hours
their task was completed and everything in sufficient
forwardness to commence the assault — but
the besiegers hesitated. They bethought them-

---

[1] Champlain's *Voyages* (ed. of 1619), in the Narrative of his
Expedition of 1615. See, also, Le Clercq, vol. I, pp. 79-87.
This Récollet writer, although having access to manuscripts of
the time of Champlain, gives but few additional facts concerning
the attack.

selves of the promised assistance of the five hundred Carantouannais, whose help, at this critical juncture, would be invaluable. Would it not be policy to await their coming? for, on that very day, they were expected. "Not being at the rendezvous as directed," says Champlain, "and as they had promised,[1] our savages were much troubled."

It was the belief, however, of Champlain that the Hurons, with the aid of his Frenchmen, were sufficiently numerous to capture the town without other assistance. "Delays are dangerous," he reasoned — "if not in all things, at least in many;" so he urged the Indians to the attack, as he plainly saw the enemy, having become aware of the strength of the besiegers and, of course, of the presence of white men with fire-arms, had begun to barricade themselves. The advice was convincing to the Hurons and they resolved at once to assault the stockade of the Onondagas.

Now the attack began. The strongest warriors to the number of two hundred seized upon the improvised wooden tower with unwonted energy, and carried it to the stockade, planting it a few feet off. Then three Frenchmen, armed with arquebuses, mounted upon it, and being well protected from the arrows and stones that could be shot or hurled at them, opened a raking fire along the galleries inside the palisades, thronged with naked and whooping defenders. Arrows of the

[1] Of course, in this, Champlain's memory is at fault; for the Carantouannais had not "promised" anything; as there had been no communication between them and the Hurons since Brulé and the twelve savages with him left the vicinity of Lake Simcoe.

Onondagas were rained upon the besiegers and sometimes with effect; stones, too, flew thick and fast against the Hurons; nevertheless, a hot fire from the tower caused the enemy to dislodge and abandon their galleries, contenting themselves afterward to fight under cover.

Then it was that Champlain expected the movable parapets that had been constructed would be brought forward as he had directed, under the cover of one of which fire was to be set to the stockade; but the excitement proved too much for such work on the part of his Hurons. They soon abandoned the parapets and "began to scream at their enemies" and shoot their arrows into the midst of them, over the palisades. And the fire that was kindled was upon the wrong side of the pickets — the wind blew the flames away from them. The besiegers soon sought to remedy this by carrying more wood; but not enough was gathered to effect anything worth mentioning, as the besieged poured an abundance of water upon the flames to extinguish them. Meanwhile, so great was the disorder and confusion among the Hurons that Champlain's orders could not be heard by them, or if heard, no attention whatever was given to the commands which he shouted in their ears. He entreated — he remonstrated — but nothing could put a stop to the wild uproar; so he, "seeing that shouting would only burst his head," wisely concluded to let his ungovernable allies take their own way, while he and his Frenchmen would do what they could in a civilized manner and fire upon such of the enemy as they could see,— with the result, he declares, of killing and maiming many of the enemy. The attack continued for three hours, the Hurons having two chiefs and about fifteen common warriors wounded, when they retreated — a disorderly rabble — to their fortified camp, Champlain himself having received two arrow wounds — one in the leg and the other in the knee, causing him much inconvenience and pain.

Now it was that the besiegers began to talk of a retreat without farther fighting, while Champlain was urging them again to assault the stronghold of the Onondagas; however, after explaining their situation, having already so many wounded to care for, they agreed to wait four days longer for the coming of the five hundred Carantouannais, and if they arrived, they would make a second attempt and would endeavor to execute his orders better than in the first attack.

On the first and second days thereafter, there prevailed a very strong wind, which would have made it an easy matter, in Champlain's opinion, to set fire to the enemy's stockade; but the Hurons could not be prevailed upon to make the attempt, pleading their wounded as an excuse. The days which passed in waiting for the arrival of the Carantouannais were enlivened by frequent skirmishes between the contending forces; and in some of these the white men found it necessary to go to the rescue of their allies. Finally, on October 16th, the five hundred warriors from Carantouan not having made their appearance, the retreat of the Hurons began,[1] their wounded, in-

---

[1] "They [Champlain's savage allies] were ready, however, to renew the onset, if Brulé and his five hundred Andastes [that is, Carantouannais] should come to their assistance. Brulé was

cluding Champlain, being carried in a kind of basket made for the occasion, each borne on the back of a strong warrior. The Onondagas followed the retiring host a short distance, when they gave up the pursuit, as they had not taken (and doubtless were convinced they could not take) any prisoners of the Hurons. Finally, the place was reached where the invaders had concealed their canoes on the shore of Lake Ontario and all were found intact.[1]

Champlain succeeded in getting safely back to Cahiagué, at the end of the year. Before returning to the St. Lawrence, he visited the Tionnontates, a nation known to the French, generally, as Nation

three days away among the villages of that people, who had not yet finished their revelries at the prospect of punishing the Iroquois. Brulé proved powerless to move them on."— Winsor: *Cartier to Frontenac*, pp. 118, 119. However, he finally succeeded, as will be seen, but when it was too late.

[1] The following is copied from the Index to Champlain's map ("Carte de la nouuelle France") of 1632, concerning the Onondaga village which Champlain failed to capture: "89. Village renfermé de 4 pallisades ou le Sieur de Champlain fut à la guerre contre les Antouhonorons où il fut pris plusieurs prisoniers sauvages." [Village enclosed within 4 palisades, where the Sieur de Champlain was during the war upon the Antouhonorons, and where numerous savages were made prisoners.] The last seven words of this extract are a sufficient evidence that Champlain had no hand in making at least a portion of the Index to his map of 1632. Where the Onondaga stronghold is pictured on his map, there is inserted the number "89," as given above.

The Iroquois fort, from a sketch by Champlain himself to be found in his *Voyages* of 1619, has been many times reproduced, both in French and English books; so, also, has his large map of 1632, given in the edition of his work of that year, but drawn by him in 1629.

du Petun, that is, Tobacco nation.[1] He also went to the country of the Cheveux Relevés,[2] some of whom, it will be remembered, he met when journeying to the Hurons from the St. Lawrence.

It was upon this visit that Champlain first heard of the Attiwandarons, to whom, for the reason of their observing, as before related, a neutral policy as to the Hurons and Iroquois, he gave the name of Neutrals. He was very desirous of visiting this nation, but was dissuaded from so doing by the Cheveux Relevés, who informed him that, at the attack on the Onondaga stronghold in the Iroquois country the year before, one of his men had killed a Neutral; and that because of this, it would be dangerous to go among them. So he returned to the Hurons the same way he went. He afterward came upon a party of Nipissings who had wintered in that country and who had promised to conduct him farther on in the prosecution of his plans and explorations, by guiding him to the northward and northwestward, to the head of Lake Huron, when, after going not a great distance, as he believed, he would reach the North Sea, but which, in reality, was Lake Superior. However, a quarrel sprung up between the Hurons and some Algonquins who were with them; and, because of this, it had been determined by the Nipissings to break off the journey to the north. "If ever," says Champlain, "a person

---

[1] South of the Nottawasaga bay, and about two days' journey west of the Huron towns, were situated nine or ten villages of the Petuns. They did not form a league with the Hurons until 1640. The languages of the two nations were nearly identical.

[2] Afterward known as Ottawas.

was greatly disheartened it was myself, since I had been waiting to see this year the North Sea, which during many preceding years I had been seeking for with great toil and effort, through many fatigues and risks of life."

Champlain, realizing now that it would be impossible to make the tour to the north, comforted himself as best he could, resolving to see that region, if possible, in a short time, although now thwarted in his designs. He had obtained so much information that he could not doubt what the savages told him of the country; and particularly, as they went to traffic with the people there,— nearly all of whom, he was informed, lived in a region where there was an abundance of game, and where there were great numbers of large animals, presumably buffaloes. He was assured that fishing was abundant there; and that the journey required forty days in going to that country, and the same length of time in returning from it. Undoubtedly, the region referred to was the southern part of the present Wisconsin and the northern portions of what is now the State of Illinois.

It was also learned by Champlain that the people of the Ottawa river and those living towards the south after leaving the French river (nearly all of whom he had visited) had little knowledge of the inhabitants to the westward of Lake Huron beyond those they traded with, as they were at war with them. "We can not," he says, "obtain better information of them, except what had been told by some prisoners — that the people of those distant countries were like Frenchmen in color and in other respects." Of course, these stories had no foundation in fact, but Champlain was inclined to believe them true — to this extent, that they were people more civilized than the savages he was then with.

After leaving word with the Hurons for Brulé, upon his return from Carantouan, to proceed northward and explore the country towards the head of Lake Huron, Champlain started for the St. Lawrence. On July 11th, 1616, he reached Quebec, to the great joy of all the people.[1]

"The courage, endurance, and heroism of Champlain were tested in the . . . . exploration of 1615. It extended from Montreal, the whole length of the Ottawa, to Lake Nipissing, the Georgian bay, [Lake] Simcoe, the system of small lakes on the south, across the Ontario, and finally ending in the interior of the State of New York, a journey through tangled forests and broken watercourses of more than a thousand miles, occupying nearly a year, executed in the face of physical suffering and hardship before which a nature less

---

[1] Brief accounts of Champlain's journey of 1615 and 1616 have frequently been given in English: see *History of the Discovery of the Northwest, by John Nicolet, in 1634,* pp. 18-20; Warburton's *Conquest of Canada,* vol. I, p. 88; O. H. Marshall, in *The Magazine of American History,* vol. I, pp. 1-5; J. G. Shea, in *The Pennsylvania Magazine of History and Biography,* vol. II, pp. 103-108; Parkman's *Pioneers of France in the New World,* pp. 357-386; Brodhead's *History of the State of New York* (Revised ed.), vol. I, pp. 67-71; Lossing's *Empire State,* p. 18; Rev. Edmund F. Slafter's "Champlain," in Winsor's *Narrative and Critical History of America,* vol. IV, pp. 124-126; Winsor's *Cartier to Frontenac,* pp. 116-121; and other works. But the most lengthy one is that published in vol. III, pp. 89-188, of the *Prince Society Publications of Champlain's "Voyages,"* being a full translation of Champlain's Narrative of 1615, by Charles Pomeroy Otis, with Historical Illustrations by Slafter.

intrepid and determined, less loyal to his great purpose, less generous and unselfish, would have yielded at the outset."[1]

But what of Brulé and the five hundred Carantouannais? They had left Carantouan; they had marched northward, leaving, probably, the territory now included in Tioga county, New York, and going through that of the present counties of Tompkins, Cayuga, Cortland and into Onondaga, but reaching the rendezvous (fixed upon near Lake Simcoe by the Hurons) two days after the departure of Champlain and his allies.[2] There was now no alternative: they must return as they came;[3] and of course Brulé was obliged to go back with them to Carantouan.[4]

---

[1] Rev. E. F. Slafter, in *Memoir of Samuel de Champlain*— vol. I, pp. 199, 200, of *Prince Society Publications of Champlain's "Voyages."*

[2] Champlain, in his Narrative of 1618, gives an erroneous reason for the retreat of the Hurons from the vicinity of the Onondaga village: "They [the Carantouannais] did not succeed in arriving until two days after our departure from that place [the Onondaga stronghold], which we were forced to abandon, since *we were too weak and worn by the inclemency of the weather* [the italicising is mine] to longer remain."

It is doubtful whether the Carantouannais determined by their reconnoitering of the deserted camp of the Hurons that they had been gone two days. It is probable that Brulé subsequently gave to Champlain the date of their arrival, which the latter readily saw was, as he gives in his Narrative of 1618, two days after he and his Hurons broke camp.

[3] Doubtless, Carantouan was the nearest of the three villages of the Carantouannais to the Onondaga stronghold, as it was a *short* three days' journey thence to the enemy's village — the objective point of Champlain and his Hurons; whereas it was a *good* three days' journey from the Carantouannais, if their three villages are considered together.

[4] "This [the Carantouannais not finding their allies at the

rendezvous] caused Brulé and the five hundred men *whom he brought* to withdraw and return to their village of Carantouan," is Champlain's declaration in his Narrative of 1618 (the italicising is mine). But, in this, he gives altogether too much authority to Brulé.

"The army of five hundred men, which Stephen Brulé was to accompany from the Susquehanna district to coöperate with Champlain in his attack on the Onondaga Fort, did not arrive before that stout palisade till two days after the retreat of the Hurons with the wounded French leader; they, too, retired, but kept up the war till they were totally conquered by the Iroquois."— John Gilmary Shea, in *The Pennsylvania Magazine of History and Biography*, vol. II, p. 108. In this, Mr. Shea expresses the correct idea as to one object of Brulé's visit to Carantouan; which was, for him, after urging the Carantouannais quickly to assemble and hasten the departure of the five hundred, to *accompany them* to the place agreed upon near the Onondaga fort.

CHAPTER VI.

BRULÉ EXPLORES THE SUSQUEHANNA AND CHESAPEAKE COUNTRY TO THE OCEAN.

We left Brulé at Carantouan, whither he had returned with the five hundred Carantouannais in the latter half of October, 1615.[1] For lack of company and escort back to the Huron villages, he must needs remain at Carantouan during the winter, —but not, of course, to continue idle within the palisaded home of his savage friends. His mission was one, as already explained, largely for an examination of their country; but he would not, certainly, be limited even to that if ulterior regions promised rich fields for visitations. So having busied himself in the vicinity in calling upon friendly Indians, for awhile, he turned his longing eyes to the southward; for he had learned, doubtless, that the Susquehanna was a stream of great length and that the country watered by it was the home of several savage tribes. He resolved, therefore, to see what (at least to him) was an unknown

---

[1] As Champlain in his *Voyages* (ed. of 1619) has been depended upon for the leading incidents in the career of Brulé after starting with the twelve savages from the Huron country for Carantouan until his return to that village with the five hundred Carantouannais in an ineffectual attempt to succor Champlain while fighting the Onondagas,— so, also, we must look to the same work for the main facts concerning the interpreter's discoveries and explorations immediately following those events. How Champlain came into possession of these facts will hereafter be narrated.

valley; and he soon started upon his perilous journey. His adventure was undertaken for no other purpose than exploration. Was the Susquehanna, from the present northern limits of Pennsylvania to the south boundary line of that State, and for some distance below, a wholly undiscovered river at that time? And had any white man previously explored to any extent the territory now included within the limits of the State of Pennsylvania? These are questions now to be answered.

The North Branch of the Susquehanna rises in Otsego county, New York, and is the outlet of Otsego and Schuyler lakes. The part of this stream which is included in that State is usually called the Susquehanna. It runs southwestward to Great Bend, in Pennsylvania, from which it returns into New York and intersects the counties of Broome and Tioga. Turning next to the left, it enters Bradford county, Pennsylvania, and runs southeastward to the coal mines of the Wyoming valley. Below Pittston it runs southwestward through Luzerne and Columbia counties to Northumberland.

The West Branch rises on the west slope of the Alleghany mountains, and drains Clearfield county and intersects Clinton and Lycoming counties. Its general direction is eastward. It is nearly two hundred and fifty miles long, and is inferior to the North Branch. It unites with the North Branch at Northumberland, forming the Susquehanna proper.

The Susquehanna from Northumberland runs southward to Harrisburg and before it reaches that city forms the boundary between Dauphin and Perry counties. Below Harrisburg it flows nearly southeastward, and forms the boundary between the counties of Lancaster and York. Passing next into Maryland, it separates Cecil county from Harford county and enters the north end of Chesapeake bay at Havre de Grace. The Susquehanna is about one hundred and fifty miles in length; but if the North Branch is included, it is five hundred miles long. It traverses a hilly, fertile and picturesque country, but its navigation is obstructed by rocky rapids. Its principal tributary is the Juniata, flowing into the parent stream from the westward.

Chesapeake bay is a large and important body of water in Maryland and Virginia, extending from the mouth of the Susquehanna river southward to Hampton Roads, and communicating with the Atlantic Ocean by a wide channel between Cape Charles and Cape Henry. It is nearly two hundred miles long, and varies in width from four to forty miles, dividing Maryland into two parts, called the eastern and western shore, and having also upon its eastern shore the counties of Accomack and Northampton in Virginia. The land on each side of the bay is deeply indented by numerous inlets or estuaries, through which the Potomac, Patuxent, Rappahannock, York, Choptank, Nanticoke, and other rivers enter the bay. The water is so deep that the largest ships can ascend it almost to the mouth of the Susquehanna. Baltimore is on an estuary which is virtually a part of the Chesapeake.

For the purposes of historical illustration, the North Branch and the Susquehanna proper may be considered as one. The Carantouannais, living in a region three good days' journey *south* of the Onondaga country, must have had their villages, therefore, on the waters of the Susquehanna. This is conceded by all writers who have had their attention directed to the subject.[1]

Following close upon the voyage of Verrazzano in 1524 was that of Stephen Gomez, who, it seems, discovered, on Saint Antony's day (June 13th), 1525, the river subsequently rediscovered by Hudson and now known by his name. Gomez was a Portuguese in the employ of Spain; but he returned to Corunna, whence he had sailed, within less than a year, having a cargo of furs and Indians — the latter for the slave-market. There is no account of his having penetrated into the interior country, north, west, or to the southwest, from the Hudson.[2]

The bay of "Santa Maria" (Chesapeake bay) was early known to the Spaniards, it having been discovered by them between the years 1524 and 1540. In 1556, an attempt was made by people of the same nationality to form a settlement in that region, which, however, proved a failure.[3] Again in 1570 was another trial; but this one, in the

---

[1] "This tribe [the Carantouannais] was probably situated on the upper waters of the Susquehanna:" *Slafter*. "The Carantouannais . . . living in three towns near the Susquehanna, were to coöperate with the Hurons:" *Shea*.

[2] Bancroft's *History of the United States* (ed. of 1890), vol. I, pp. 26, 27. Consult, in this connection, Winsor's *Narrative and Critical History of America*, vol. III, pp. 16.— vol. IV, pp. 9–11, 28–30, 413, 414. The river, generally believed to have been the Hudson which was discovered by Gomez, was called the "Rio de San Antonio."

[3] Sharf's *History of Maryland*, vol. I, p. 22.

end, met with no better success.[1] Three years after, Pedro Menendez Morquez sailed into the bay, estimated the distance between its headlands, took soundings of the water in its channel, and observed that it had " many rivers and harbors on both sides" in which vessels might anchor.[2] Did he discover the Susquehanna where it enters the bay? Probably such was not the fact. He explored none of the streams he saw, nor did he give names to any. It is safe to conclude, therefore, that, as yet, the Susquehanna was a river unknown to civilized man.

An attempt in 1585 by Englishmen to form a colony on the coast of what is now North Carolina, although not successful, resulted the next year in making known to England for the first time the bay already visited by Marquez. But two other colonies, together taking the name of Virginia, were, farther to the northward, subsequently more fortunate. Three English vessels, carrying one hundred and five emigrants, in April, 1607, reached the Chesapeake; and soon Jamestown was founded by one of the companies organized to settle Virginia. The guiding spirit of the new settlement was Captain John Smith. On June 2nd, 1608, he left Jamestown with fourteen others " to perform his discovery " of the bay of " Chisapeack" (Chesapeake). After finishing a part of his proposed work, he returned, reaching the

[1] For a readable account of this attempt to form a settlement at a place called "Axacan," see *Historical Register*, vol. I, pp. 114–120. But the proposition there set forth, that "Axacan" might have been located on the Susquehanna, is entitled to no consideration.

[2] Sharf's *History of Maryland*, vol. I, pp. 22, 23.

settlement on the 21st of July. Three days thereafter he again started, this time with twelve men, to complete his discoveries. As, however, only so much of his second voyage as has an immediate bearing on his reaching the mouth of the Susquehanna river is of special importance to our narrative, his record, which he afterwards published, will be given, but restricted to a small portion of his recital of all that he saw and heard during his absence. He sailed in a barge of "hardly 2 toons," using oars and a sail.

"The wind being contrary," says Smith, "caused our stay two or three days at Kecoughton [now Hampton, Virginia]: the King feasted us with much mirth; his people were persuaded we went purposely to be revenged of the Massawomeks [Mohawks or other Iroquois]. In the evening, we fired a few rockets, which, flying in the air, so terrified the poor savages, they supposed nothing impossible we attempted, and desired to assist us.

"The first night we anchored at Stingray isle. The next day crossed Patawomeks [Potomac] river, and hastened to the river Bolus [Patapsco river]. We went not much further before we might see the [Chesapeake] bay to divide in two heads, and arriving there we found it divided into four, all which we searched so far as we could sail them. Two of them we found inhabited."

After leaving the Patapsco, the next river discovered by Smith was the Susquehanna. However, he could not ascend the stream with his boat two miles for rocks.[1]

---

[1] "At the end of the [Chesapeake] Bay, where it is 6 or 7 myles in breadth, it divides itself into 4 branches, the best com-

"Near it [the Susquehanna]," are the words of Smith, " north and by west runneth a creek a mile and a half, at the head whereof the ebb [tide] left us on shore, where we found many trees cut with hatchets. The next tide, keeping the shore to seek for some savages (for within thirty leagues' sailing we saw not any — being a barren country), we went up another small river [now known as Bush river], like a creek, six or seven miles."[1] Returning down this stream, the Captain set sail to cross the bay, when he unexpectedly encountered " seven or eight canoes full of Massawomeks [Mohawks or other Iroquois],— we seeing them prepare to assault us, left our oars and made way with our sails to encounter them, yet were we but five with our Captain that could stand, for within two days after we left Kecoughtan, the rest (being all of the last supply) were sick almost to death, until they were seasoned to the country. Having shut them under our tarpaulin, we put their hats upon sticks by the barge's side, and betwixt two hats a man with two pieces, to make us seem

meth Northwest from among the mountains, but though Canows may goe a dayes iourney or two vp it, we could not get two myles vp it with our boat for rockes."— Smith's *Génerall Historie of Virginia, New England & the Summer Isles* (London: 1624), p. 24. Arber's Reprint (1884), p. 349. (I have thought it best, in the text, generally to modernize Smith's spelling.)

This *Génerall Historie of Virginia*, etc., gives an account of the infant colony begun, as we have seen, in 1607. Smith's book also contains a supplementary narrative of his trip to the Susquehanna river, prepared by three of his companions. The work, as a whole, contains two hundred and forty-eight pages. To it was added a *Map of Virginia*, which had been previously published. (See Appendix to our Narrative, Note XIII.)

[1] Ibid.

many, and so we think the Indians supposed these hats to be men, for they fled with all possible speed to the shore, and there staid, staring at the sailing of our barge till we anchored right against them. Long it was ere we could draw them to come to us. At last they sent two of their company unarmed in a canoe, the rest all followed to second them if need required. These two being but each presented with a bell, brought aboard all their fellows, presenting our captain with venison, bears' flesh, fish, bows, arrows, clubs, targets, and bear skins. We understood them nothing at all, but by signs whereby they signified unto us they had been at war with the Tockwoghes [on what is now known as the Sassafras river, Maryland], the which they confirmed by showing us their green [fresh] wounds, but the night parting us, we imagined they appointed the next morning to meet [us], but after that we never saw them."[1]

"The next day," continues Smith, "we discovered the small river and people of Tockwhogh trending eastward."[2]

And thus again the Captain: "Entering the river Tochwogh [now known as the Sassafras river] the savages all armed, in a fleet of boats, after their barbarous manner, round environed us;

[1] "He [Smith] was the first to publish to the English the power of the Mohawks, 'who dwelt upon a great water, and had many boats and many men,' and, as it seemed to the feebler Algonkin tribes, 'made war upon all the world;' in the Chesapeake, he encountered a fleet of their canoes."—Bancroft's *United States* (ed. of 1890), vol. I, p. 94.

[2] Smith's spelling of the name of the Indian tribe with whom the "Massawomeks" had been at war is not uniform. He writes "Tockwogh," "Tockwhogh," and, sometimes, "Tochwogh." The pronunciation was, probably, *tock-wock*.

so it chanced one of them could speak the language of Powhatan [the celebrated Indian chief, whose daughter was Pocahontas] who persuaded the rest to friendly parley. But when they saw us furnished with the Massawomeks weapons, and we faining the invention of Kecoughtan [that the party was going against the Massawomeks] to have taken them by force, they conducted us to their palisaded town, manteled with the barks of trees, with scaffolds like mounts, breasted about with breasts very formally. Their men, women and children, with dances, songs, fruits, furs, and what they had, kindly welcomed us, spreading mats for us to sit on, stretching their best abilities to express their loves. Many hatchets, knives, pieces of iron and brass, we saw amongst them, which they reported to have from the Sasquesahannocks, a mighty people and mortal enemies with the Massawomeks [Mohawks or other Iroquois]."[1]

From the savage Tockwoghs, then, Smith heard, for the first time, of the Susquehanna In-

[1] "On the east side of the bay is the river Tockwhogh, and upon it a people that can make 100 men, seated some seaven myles within the river; where they have a fort very well pallisadaed and mantelled with barkes of trees."— *Smith*.

"Through Smith's interpreter," says Prof. Guss (*Historical Register*, vol. I, pp. 120, 121), "who understood English, and Powhatan Algonquin, he [Smith] found no difficulty in communicating with the Tockwocks."

But Smith had no interpreter who was an Indian that could understand English. The Captain understood some "Powhatan," and managed to hold conversation with the "Tockwock," who, *it chanced*, could speak the same language;— that is, "Powhatan Algonquin," as Prof. Guss terms it. It is evident the Tockwoghs were of Iroquois lineage—not "Tockwock Algonquins," as that writer would term them.

dians. These savages were "seated 2 daies higher" on the Susquehanna "than was passage for the discoverers Barge."¹ It was resolved by Smith to return to the mouth of that river, and if possible hold a council with the "Sasquesahanocks." Thereupon the party again set sail.

The Tockwogh Indian who could speak the language of Powhatan (of which language Smith had some knowledge), and who was with the white men in the barge, was prevailed upon to go among the "Sasquesahanocks" to persuade them to make the journey, taking with him another Indian of his own nation who could also assist in the work. "We prevailed," says the Captain, "with the interpreter to take with him another interpreter, to persuade the Sasquesahanocks to come visit us, for their languages are different. Three or four days we expected their return, then sixty of those giant-like people came down, with presents of venison, tobacco pipes three foot in length, baskets, targets, bows and arrows."²

Taking with him in his barge five of the "Sasquesahanock" chiefs ("werowances," as they were called), and leaving the rest of the savages at the mouth of the river, with their canoes, "the winds being so high they durst not passe," Smith again spread his sail to cross the bay to the Sassafras ("Tockwhogh") river.

In the "pallizadoed towne" of the Tockwoghs,

---

¹ See Appendix, Note XIII.

² That the language of the Tockwoghs was "different" from the "Sasquesahanocks" does not necessarily imply that it was radically different — that the two nations could not have been of the same linguistic stock.

Smith and his companions were highly entertained with the strange manners of the "Sasquesahanocks:" "Our order," is the quaint language of Smith, "was daily to have prayer, with a psalm, at which solemnity the poor savages much wondered, our prayers being done, a while they were busied with a consultation till they had contrived their business. They then began in a most passionate manner to hold up their hands to the sun, with a most fearful song, then embracing our Captain, they began to adore him in like manner: though he rebuked them, yet they proceeded till their song was finished: which done with a most strange furious action, and a hellish voice; began an oration of their loves; that ended, with a great painted bear-skin they covered him; then one ready with a great chain of white beads, weighing at least six or seven pounds hung it about his neck, the others had eighteen mantels, made of divers sorts of skins sewed together; all these with many other toyes they laid at his feet, stroking their ceremonious hands about his neck for his creation to be their governor and protector, promising their aid, victuals, or what they had to be his, if he would stay with them, to defend and revenge them of the Massawomeks. But we left them at Tockwhogh, sorrowing for our departure, yet we promised the next year again to visit them."

But Smith did not leave the "Sasquesahanocks" and the Tockwoghs until he had obtained from the former the important information that the hatchets, knives, and other articles of European manufacture possessed by their nation had been obtained from the French on (as the Captain understood them) the River St. Lawrence. There had been such a trade carried on by way of the West Branch of the Susquehanna, thence across to Lake Erie and down the Niagara river, thence along the shores of Lake Ontario and down the St. Lawrence, for several years, with transient fur-traders in the last-mentioned river, and with others more permanently located below.[1]

The failure of Smith and his men to ascend in their barge the Susquehanna river farther than about two miles left all the extensive region afterward included within the boundaries of Pennsylvania unexplored by civilized man. And for the next eight years and more, so far as known, no Englishman passed within its limits, as now defined. The English explorers of the Chesapeake bay had, as we have just narrated, reached a point within a few miles of what became afterward (and still is) its southern boundary—"Mason and Dixon's Line."[2]

As early as 1597, voyages were undertaken from Holland to America. In 1608, Henry Hudson, an Englishman, offered his services to the Dutch East India Company to undertake a search for a north-

[1] This fact is to be inferred from what is said by Champlain in his *Voyages* of 1613. See, also, in this connection (as to this grand détour having been made by the savages), Appendix to our Narrative, Note XII. The great circuit, as already explained, was followed to avoid the hostile Iroquois. It was this round-about way, in going from the mouth of the Niagara river to the Susquehanna, that Brulé could not take for want of time.

[2] See Appendix, Note XIII. What is said by Smith in Chapter VI, of his "First Book" concerning his visit to the head of the Chesapeake, must be read in connection with his summary account and description in his "Second Book:" they must be construed together.

east passage to China, and they were accepted. On April 4th, 1609, a vessel of about eighty tons' burden, commanded by him and manned by Netherlanders and Englishmen, set sail. His yacht was named the *Half Moon*. Failing to the northward and northeastward, he turned his prow to the westward and southwestward. Early in July, he reached the banks of Newfoundland; and, soon after the beginning of September, he rediscovered the river which afterwards received his name. Now, for a while, Dutch voyages to the east coast of America were given up, to be renewed, however, in 1613, by Henry Christiansen in the *Fortune* and Adrian Block in the *Tiger*. These navigators were instructed to sail for the island of Manhattan and to renew and continue their traffic with the savages along the Hudson (then called the Mauritius) river,—the two having previously, in one ship, visited that stream and obtained furs from the natives. By accident, the *Tiger* was burned at Manhattan while Block was preparing to return to Holland, but its commander was not discouraged. During the winter of 1613–14, he built a small yacht, erecting a few huts on the island for his accommodation while engaged in the work. But this was not the beginning of New York city, for it again lapsed into "primeval solitude."[1]

By the spring of 1614, other vessels had arrived from Holland at Manhattan, and it was perceived that to secure the largest returns from the fur trade, a factor should reside permanently near the

[1] Martha J. Lamb's *History of the City of New York*, vol. I, p. 35.

Mohawks on the west side of the Hudson and contiguous also to the Mohicans on the east side of the river; so Christiansen erected a trading house on " Castle Island" at the west side of the stream, a little below the present city of Albany. To the small post was immediately given the name of " Fort Nassau." [1]

By October 11th of the year last mentioned, so much had the trade increased to the Hudson, that a company was chartered giving the members a special trading license to " New Netherland," as the region therein, for the first time, was called — " exclusively to visit and navigate to the aforesaid newly-discovered lands lying in America, between New France and Virginia, the sea-coasts whereof extend from the fortieth to the forty-fifth degree of latitude, now named New Netherland, for four voyages within the period of three years, commencing on January 1st, 1615, next ensuing, or sooner." But not until some time in the year 1616 as a result of the presence of the Dutch in "New Netherland" had any of these traders reached what is now the State of Pennsylvania.

During the year 1615, the Dutch at Fort Nassau, up the Hudson, continued, it is true, actively employed in prosecuting a quiet traffic with the Mohawks and Mohicans, near that post; and there were doubtless scouting-parties exploring the country to the westward of Manhattan, but none pene-

---

[1] Brodhead's *History of the State of New York* (Revised Ed.), vol. I, pp. 54, 55, 755, 756. Mrs. Lamb, in her work cited in the previous note, errs in giving (p. 42) the date of the founding of Fort Nassau as of 1615.

trated so far as actually to reach the lower or even middle portions of the Delaware river, where dwelt the Minquas, a nation of linguistic affinity with the Iroquois, or Five Nations, as before mentioned, but their deadly enemies and known to the latter as " Ogehage."[1]

It is reasonably certain that in 1614 the Carantouannais were at peace with all the tribes with which the Dutch were trading except the Mohawks; with the latter, a bitter war was raging as with all the other nations forming the league or confederacy known to the French afterwards as the Iroquois. It is highly probable, therefore, that the three Dutch prisoners taken in 1614 by the Carantouannais (but delivered up because they were supposed to be Frenchmen) were, at the time of their capture, engaged with the Mohawks, having joined the latter from Fort Nassau, up the Hudson. As the war was doubtless carried on to the northeastward of Carantouan, it is not at all likely that these Dutchmen, while on the war-path with the " Maquaas " (Mohawks), saw any portion of what is now the territory included within the boundaries of the State of Pennsylvania. The way, then, was clear-

[1] These Minquas were Southern Iroquois (see Appendix, Note XV), and the very next year (1616) they captured three Dutch explorers, who, however, were soon given up. These Dutchmen were from Fort Nassau up the Hudson, and had gone down the Delaware early in the season to about the locality of the present city of Philadelphia, when they were made prisoners by the Minquas. That they went so far on the river before being captured is strong evidence that the Carantouannais were not located on the upper portions of it. (Consult, in this connection, E. B. O'Callighan's *Documents Relating to the Colonial History of the State of New York*, vol. I, pp. 13, 14; also, Brodhead's *History of the State of New York* (Revised Ed.), vol. I, pp. 78, 79).

ly open, in the autumn of 1615, for Brulé to become its first explorer (if, indeed, he was not the first white man to set foot upon its soil); and that he succeeded in the enterprise, there can be no reasonable doubt.

"Brulé," says Champlain in speaking of how his interpreter spent the winter after his return from the Onondaga fort to Carantouan, "made a tour along a river that flows in the direction of Florida, where are many powerful and warlike nations, carrying on wars against each other. The climate there is very temperate, and there are a great number of animals and abundance of small game. But to traverse and reach these regions requires patience, on account of the difficulties involved in passing the extensive wastes.

"He continued his course along the river as far as the sea, also to islands and to lands near them, which are inhabited by various and populous tribes of savages who are well disposed and love the French above all other white people. But those who know the Dutch complain severely of them, since they treat them very roughly. Among other things, he observed that the winter was very temperate, that it snowed very rarely, and that when it did the snow was not a foot deep and melted immediately.

"After traversing the country and observing what was noteworthy, he returned to the village of Carantouan, in order to find an escort for returning to our settlement [on the St. Lawrence]."[1]

The conclusion is inevitable that the "river that flows in the direction of Florida" was the Susque-

---

[1] Champlain's *Voyages* of 1618 (ed. of 1619).

hanna, along which Brulé " made a tour." From the Onondaga fort assailed by Champlain and his Hurons, a three days' journey south would bring Brulé to no other stream flowing toward Florida but that river; and such would be the fact if the stronghold just mentioned had been located a considerable distance farther to the westward than the vicinity of the present city of Syracuse, New York. It could not have been the Delaware; for the waters of this stream are to the southeastward and too distant.[1] " Brulé now returned," says a recent writer, " with them [the five hundred Carantouannais] to Carantouan, and, with enterprise worthy of his commander, spent the winter [of 1615 – 16] in a tour of exploration. Descending a river, evidently the Susquehanna, he followed it to its junction with the sea,"[2] — Champlain doubtless considering the Chesapeake, from what Brulé had narrated, an enlargement of the Susquehanna until the Atlantic was reached by him.[3]

As the savages then occupying the valley of the Susquehanna, even as far south as its mouth, were, as hereafter shown, of the same linguistic family, Brulé must have found little difficulty in conversing with them, as they all spoke dialects similar to that of the Huron, with which, as already explained, he was familiar: and as all were of the Iroquois stock, they (and including other nations

---

[1] Upon Champlain's Map of 1632, the Carantouannais are located on the Delaware — an error, which, considering the imperfect information he then had of the locality, is not at all surprising.

[2] Parkman's *Pioneers of France in the New World*, p. 378.

[3] See Appendix, Note XIV.

beyond) may, with propriety, be classified, in view of their general location, Southern Iroquois.[1]

That the Carantouannais, as we have already suggested, had a village farther down the Susquehanna valley than Carantouan, seems probable.

"At Wyoming," says a recent writer, "were the Scahentoarrunon, or People of the Great Flats; on the West Branch [of the Susquehanna] were the Otzinachson, or people of the Demons' Dens; on the Juniata were the Onojutta-Haga, or Standing Stone people; below the mountains, on the river [Susquehanna] and branches, were the Susquehannocks, extending to the Potomac river."[2]

It is only of the last mentioned that we have any particular account of immediately (as we may say) preceding the year 1615. Captain Smith's curiosity to see them, after the Tockwoghs had assured him they had obtained from them the "hatchets, knives and pieces of iron and brass" exhibited to the English, must have been great, as we would naturally suppose; hence his sending the two Tockwoghs to their homes asking them to visit him and his party at the mouth of the Susquehanna. The Captain declares the "Sasquesahanocks" "could make near six hundred able men, and are pallisaded in their towns to defend them from the Massawomeks, their mortal enemies." The location of their principal village is uncertain.[3]

[1] See Appendix, Note XV.

[2] Prof. A. L. Guss, in the *Historical Register*, vol. I, p. 42.

[3] "It is claimed," says Prof. Guss, "that this chief town [of the 'Sasquesahanocks'] was always near the mouth of Conestoga creek. As we know that the location of such Indian towns were often changed . . . and as we know there was a 'Sasque-

"Sixty of these Sasquesahanocks," says Smith (we modernize his spelling), "came to us with skins, bows, arrows, targets, beads, swords, and tobacco pipes for presents. Such great and well-proportioned men are seldom seen, for they seemed like giants to the English, yea and to the neighbors [the Tockwoghs], yet seemed of an honest and simple disposition, with much ado restrained from adoring us as gods.

"These are the strangest people of all these countries, both in language and attire; for their language it may well become their proportions, sounding from them as a voice in a vault. Their attire is the skins of bears and wolves, some have cossacks made of bears' heads and skins that a man's head goes through the skins and neck, and the ears of the bear fastened to his shoulders, the nose and teeth hanging down his breast, another bear's split behind him, and at the end of the nose hung a paw, the half sleeves coming to the elbows were the necks of bears, and the arms through the mouth with paws hanging at their noses. One had the head of a wolf hanging in a chain for a jewel, his tobacco pipe three-quarters of a yard long, prettily carved with a bird, a deer, or some such devise at the great end, sufficient to beat out

hannocks new town' where 'some falls below hinder navigation,' about 1648; and that 'the present Sasquahana Fort,' in 1670, was on the southside of the river below the 'greatest fal,' now known as the Conewago Falls; and as they had a fort at the mouth of the Octoraro, perhaps as early as 1662, it is impossible to exactly locate the town designated by Smith."—*Historical Register*, vol. I, p. 165. It will be noticed, however, that Smith declares they, the "Sasquesahanocks," had more than one palisaded town.

one's brains: with bows, arrows and clubs suitable to their greatness."

"On the east side of the [Chesapeake]," continues Smith, "is the river Tockwogh [now, as before explained, known as the Sassafras river], and upon it a people that can make one hundred men, seated some seven miles within the river [that is — up from its mouth]: where they have a fort very well palisaded and manteled with barks of trees. Next them is Ozinies with sixty men." The nation below the one last named was the "Kuscarawaocks" (afterward known as the "Nanticokes"), "a people with two hundred men." Farther down were the Wighcocomicos (Wicomicos), "a people with one hundred men." And of two nations still farther south on the same side of the bay Smith says: "But they [who] are on the river Acohanock with forty men, and they of [the] Accomack [with] eighty men, doth equalize [equal] any [of those in] the territories of Powhatan, and speak his language,— who over all these doth rule as king."[1]

It is evident that not only the "Sasquesahanocks" but the "Tockwoghs" were of Iroquois stock (for both stockaded their towns);[2] while the other nations below on the east side of the bay

[1] Smith's *Générall Historie of Virginia*, p. 5. Arber's Reprint, p. 350. It seems highly probable that the estimate of Smith as to the number of men of each nation was restricted to the town visited by him. His estimate of the "Sasquesahanocks" was probably with reference to their principal town only, from their report.

[2] Prof. Guss (in the *Historical Register*, vol. I, pp. 120, 121), thinks the "Tockwoghs" were Algonquin: "The Tockwocks were most probably a branch of the Nanticokes, but possibly

were (unless the "Ozinies" be excepted) Algonquins. But Brulé could have had no difficulty in talking with any or all these people, as he could hold converse equally well with those of Iroquois or Algonquin lineage.

So many of the Southern Iroquois as were visited by Brulé were doubtless told by him of the aid the French were giving the Hurons, the allies of the Carantouannais; and this (although some may have known the fact), of course, secured kind treatment to him from all of them.

But did Brulé reach the ocean in his exploration? He told Champlain he went as far as the sea. He would not likely have mistaken Chesapeake bay for the Atlantic. He speaks, as we have seen, of islands which he visited; of these, in the bay and near by, it is well known, there are many. None could have been found had the explorer gone no farther than the mouth of the Susquehanna.[1]

Some Indians, doubtless on the Chesapeake, told Brulé that they were acquainted with white men who treated them "very roughly;" and this was repeated by Brulé to Champlain; the latter, tak-

---

Delawares, and certainly of the Algonquin family." But he forgets what he has previously written (p. 47): "The Algonquins seldom had any fortifications and then only of the rudest construction. The Iroquois generally had well palisaded towns."

[1] "Georgian Bay and the Chesapeake were thus connected by Brulé in the spring of 1616, but there were no newspapers in those days; consequently there was no fame — no eclat — around the poor explorer. He played the part of Stanley in Africa, but he added neither a title to his humble rank of interpreter, nor a penny to his purse. At the age of twenty-two, he had achieved a great Canadian work."—*Sulte.*

ing it for granted they were "Flamens" (Dutch), so reported, as we have seen, in the recital of his interpreter's story. But the Dutch, in 1615, had no traffic with the Indians upon either the Susquehanna river or Chesapeake bay. The white men then spoken of by the savages were probably the English upon the James river, who, it is well known, had for some time treated several tribes "very roughly." Champlain was ignorant of the Jamestown settlement. Brulé, therefore, could not have gone any farther than Cape Charles, unless he made a flying trip up the coast to the islands lying to the northeastward. Indeed, the time of his absence from Carantouan precludes the idea of any farther exploration by him.

So, the indomitable explorer, Brulé, having spent the winter — which was "very temperate," where "snow fell very rarely, and when it did it was not a foot deep and melted immediately"— in traveling through what is now the State of Pennsylvania — a country never before explored by a white man, in "observing what was noteworthy," and in journeying across what is now Maryland and even into the present Virginia,— returned to Carantouan for guides to conduct him back to the St. Lawrence, or at least to the country of the Hurons.[1]

[1] "Now you have the name [Brulé] of the first European who visited the vast domain which W. Penn called after his own, more than sixty years afterwards."—*Sulte*.

CHAPTER VII.

RETURN OF BRULÉ TO THE ST. LAWRENCE.—HIS REMARKABLE ESCAPE FROM TORTURE.

Brulé tarried awhile at Carantouan after having explored the Susquehanna river and Chesapeake bay, when five or six Carantouannais concluded to act as guides for him back to the Huron villages. The route taken was again through the country of the Senecas and, probably, not far from the course followed by him when he came with his twelve Hurons to the Carantouannais the year previous.[1] Again he met the enemy, but this time, having fewer protectors and the Senecas being in considerable numbers, the result was very different from the hostile meeting which took place on his journey outward. Then, it was a few Iroquois who were captured; now, it was the white man and his guides — who were forced to flee for their lives.[2]

The Senecas, seeing how few there were of the strangers, at once charged upon them,— so courageously, indeed, as to scatter the little party. There was no time for rallying, although the Carantouannais soon embodied themselves and pursued their journey without loss of life, but with-

[1] Brulé must have left Carantouan for his homeward trip about April 1st (1616).

[2] There is no information extant as to how many days the party had traveled before the enemy were discovered; it was probably not less than three or four, judging from the distance intervening between Carantouan and the Seneca country.

out Brulé, who had purposely kept away from his guides in hopes the more surely to escape from the foe. As he was now alone in the interminable woods and greatly bewildered, he could not return to Carantouan, neither could he find a trail leading in any direction whatever, nor any sign which might help him, so that he could effect his retreat back to the Carantouannais. Hopelessly he wandered about for several days with nothing to eat. The pangs of hunger were great, and he came well-nigh giving up in despair, when finally he saw a gleam of hope: it was an Indian foot-path that he had discovered, and his spirits revived.

Brulé, distressed as he was, determined to follow the trail he had found, for better or for worse — whichever way it might lead — wherever it might go — whether towards his friends or his foes; for he would rather trust to his enemies than to perish in the wilderness alone and most wretchedly, as he knew he would unless help came in some shape.[1]

There was a thought which encouraged him — he knew he could, by effort, make any Iroquois into whose hands he might fall understand what

---

[1] "When, in the spring, he [Brulé] returned to Carantouan, five or six of the Indians offered to guide him towards his countrymen. Less fortunate than before, he encountered on the way a band of Iroquois, who, rushing upon the party, scattered them through the woods. Brulé ran like the rest. The cries of pursuers and pursued died away in the distance. The forest was still around him. He was lost in the shady labyrinth. For three or four days he wandered, helpless and famished, till at length he found an Indian foot-path, and choosing between starvation and the Iroquois, desperately followed it to throw himself on their mercy [if by those Indians he should be captured]." — Parkman: *Pioneers of France in the New World*, p. 378.

he would say to them, which possibly would save his life.

It was not long that Brulé traveled upon the path before he discovered, on their way to their village, three Seneca Indians loaded with fish. He ran after them and approaching them made the depths of the forest ring with a shout, according to the custom of savages, to attract their attention. The three turned to see who had thus signaled them, when, beholding a white man, they were made afraid and would have thrown down their loads and fled had not Brulé called to them, which gave them assurance that they had nothing to fear.[1]

They laid down their bows and arrows, indicating they were not disposed to attack the stranger, and Brulé thereupon laid down his arms in token also of his being inclined to peace.[2]

Brulé, on coming up to the three savages, related to them, as well as he could, the story of his misfortune; explained to them his miserable condition,— how weak and feeble he was, not having tasted food for three or four days. Pity and com-

---

[1] "He [Brulé] soon saw three Indians in the distance, laden with fish newly caught, and called to them in the Huron tongue, which was radically similar to that of the Iroquois:" *Parkman*, loc. cit. That the fish were "newly caught," is highly probable, but Champlain does not so declare; neither does he say that Brulé called to the savages "in the Huron tongue;" such, however, was doubtless the fact, notwithstanding he (Champlain) affirms in this connection that Brulé knew how to speak their (the Iroquois) language. It is fair to presume he could only, by persevering effort, aided by signs and the use of "the Huron tongue which was radically similar" to their own, make them comprehend what he was saying.

[2] It seems altogether certain that Brulé was only armed with bow and arrows, as was each Iroquois he was now approaching.

passion were at once aroused in the breasts of the
Indians; he was offered a pipe and they smoked
together according to Indian custom. He was then
conducted to their village, where he was given
something to eat and kindly tendered every assistance in his distress.[1]

Although Brulé's guides (the five or six Carantouannais) had escaped from their enemies and
had lost their white companion, they nevertheless
proceeded on their way to the Hurons, arriving
at Cahiagué on April 22nd. They communicated
to Champlain, who was at that village, information of Brulé, whom they said they had left on the
road, he having returned, for some reason, to
Carantouan — this latter assertion being, of course,
only a guess on their part. Naturally, they believed if he escaped with his life and was not
captured he would find little difficulty in making
his way back to the place of starting.[2]

But to return to the Seneca village and to Brulé,
whose distress had so providentially been relieved.
No sooner had the savage occupants of the place

[1] It is probable that the Seneca village to which Brulé was
guided was located near the Genesee river, possibly in the present county of Livingston, New York. It seems altogether evident, because of Brulé having met hostile Iroquois near one of
their villages, that he and his guides were not returning in the
wide circuit,— the "grand detour"— which has before been
spoken of as being sometimes taken by the Carantouannais in
journeying to the Hurons.

[2] As to any farther information having been obtained from
these savages concerning his absent interpreter, Champlain is
silent. It would be strange indeed did he not question them as
to Brulé's whereabouts during the winter that had just passed
and as to the march of the five hundred Carantouannais to
aid him and his Hurons against the Onondagas, though he
seems not to have gained from them the reason for the delay.

learned that an "Adoresetoüy" had arrived (that was the name they had given the French, signifying "men of iron"), than they quickly assembled and in great numbers to see the white man. He was taken to the cabin of one of the principal chiefs, where he was closely questioned: "Whence came you? What circumstances drove you hither? How did you happen to lose your way? Do you not belong to the Adoresetoüy, who make war upon us?" To all these queries he made prompt reply; — particularly was he careful to say that he belonged to a better nation than the French, which nation was yearning to make their acquaintance and to make them their friends. But the wily savages did not believe what he said. They threw themselves upon him — they tore out his nails with their teeth — they burnt him with glowing firebrands — they plucked out his beard: all of which was contrary to the will of their chief.[1]

It is evident from Champlain's narrative of what he was told by Brulé, that the fierce Senecas had already begun the customary torture inflicted by savages upon prisoners. Brulé was a Catholic, al-

[1] "A crowd gathered about him [Brulé]. 'Whence do you come? Are you not one of the Frenchmen, the men of iron, who make war on us?' Brulé answered that he was of a nation better than the French and fast friends of the Iroquois. His captors, incredulous, tied him to a tree, tore out his beard by handfulls, and burned him with firebrands, while their chief vainly interposed in his behalf. — Parkman: *Pioneers of France in the New World*, pp. 378, 379. Champlain does not say that Brulé was tied to a tree; Sagard, who, also, as will presently be seen, had the account from the lips of Brulé some years after, says he was stretched on the ground. It will be noticed that Parkman omits mention of Brulé having had his nails torn out. He changes Champlain's words as to the plucking out of his beard "hair by hair" to "by handfulls"— which is more probable.

though, it seems, not very devout. He wore upon his breast an *Agnus Dei*, which was attached to his neck. This was now observed by one of the savages, who, after asking him what it was, at once made an attempt to seize it and pull it off. But Brulé resisted this, and with courageous words replied: "If you take it and kill me you will yourself immediately die — you and all your kin." But the Indian persisted in his "malicious purpose." However, before accomplishing his work, there came relief to the suffering white man from a source as sudden as it was unexpected.

It was a fair day — the heavens were serene — when, as unlooked for by Brulé as it was astonishing to the savages, "darkness brooded o'er the scene;" — there were great and thick clouds in the sky, and quickly followed "thunders and lightnings so violent and long-continued that it was something strange and awful." Never before had the Indians seen or heard anything like it — it was a most frightful storm. The savages were filled with terror. They lost their interest in the terrible work of putting the white man to death. They fled from him without even unbinding him; for they were now mortally afraid of him. Thereupon Brulé called in gentle words to them, making them, however, to understand that the Great Spirit was angry with them for their treatment of him.[1]

---

[1] Six years or more after relating these facts to Champlain, Brulé gave to Friar Sagard the same particulars. The latter published them in 1636, in his *History of Canada*, substantially the same as reported to Champlain. In speaking of the interpreter having become separated from his Carantouannais guides, he says in effect:

"Brulé slept several nights in the woods until one morning,

The Seneca chief now kindly unbound the prisoner, escorted him to his lodge, where he took care of him and dressed his wounds.¹ After this, there was no dance, no feast, no merry-making, to which Brulé was not invited.²

After remaining some time in the Iroquois village, Brulé determined to again start for the French settlement upon the St. Lawrence, to pursue his

having found a beaten path, he followed it, reaching a village of Iroquois, where he was immediately seized and taken prisoner, and afterwards condemned to death by their council. The poor man, very much frightened, did not know to which saint he could give himself; for, to hope for mercy, he knew very well he could not, and so he had recourse to God and to patience, and submitted himself to the Divine wishes more because he was obliged to than otherwise, for he was not devout, judging by what he told us.

"One day having found himself in great danger of death, all the prayer he said was his Benedictus, but I do not know whether he said it here. Being about to die (for already they had stretched him on the earth and were pulling out his beard), and one of the savages seeing the Agnus Dei which he carried hanging around his neck, and wanting to take it from him, Brulé began to shout and yell and told his tormentors that if they took it from him, God would punish them, as God did accordingly; for, no sooner had they put their hands on it to take it from his neck than the heavens which had been until now cloudless, grew stormy all at once and sent forth so much lightning, so much thunder, and made so much noise that the savages believed themselves to be at their last day and ran into their wigwams, leaving their prisoner alone."—(See Appendix to our Narrative, Note XXII [c], where the words of Sagard are given in French, as originally printed, and then translated with some variations from the above.)

¹ Champlain says: "The chief then approached Brulé," etc., meaning, clearly, that it was the one who was opposed to his people torturing their prisoner, and who now unbound him.

² Thus Parkman (*Pioneers of France in the New World*, p. 379): "The day was hot, and one of those thunder-gusts which often succeed the fierce heats of an American midsummer was rising against the sky. Brulé pointed to the inky clouds as

journey by way of the Huron villages.¹ The Senecas proffered guides to conduct him some distance on his way; and he was conducted by them four days, when, it is believed, the mouth of the Niagara river was reached. From this point he could not, though alone, fail in reaching in safety the Huron country and its scenes, with which he was familiar; so his guides there left him.²

Before departing from the village where he had so fortuitously escaped death by torture, Brulé assured the Iroquois he would bring about friendly relations between them and the French and their enemies, the Hurons and their allies — promising to return to them that they might swear friendship with each other.³

tokens of the anger of his God. The storm broke, and, as the celestial artillery boomed over their darkening forests, the Iroquois were stricken with a superstitious terror. All fled from the spot, leaving their victim still bound fast, until the chief who had endeavored to protect him returned, cut the cords, and leading him to his lodge dressed his wounds. Thenceforth there was neither dance nor feast to which Brulé was not invited."

¹ The exact time of his leaving is unknown, but it could not have been much before the first of June (1616).

² Assuming the Seneca village to have been not far to the eastward of the Genesee river, four days' travel would be sufficient to bring Brulé to the mouth of the Niagara, as above suggested.

³ " Brulé had an eventful life. While trying with a small party of Indians to reach the Huron country, they were attacked and scattered. Brulé at last fell in with a few Iroquois going to the fields, and endeavored to approach them in a friendly way, assuring them that he was not of the nation that had just attacked them. They treated him as a prisoner and proceeded to torture him. As they endeavored to tear a religious object from his neck, he threatened them with the vengeance of Heaven. A sudden clap of thunder with vivid lightning was to their mind a fulfillment of his threat. He was released, his wounds cured, and a party of warriors escorted him for several days."—

Brulé soon reached the Hurons[1] to find, of course, great good-will toward himself, but his patron — Champlain — had, on the twentieth of May, started back to the St. Lawrence; so he resolved to tarry with the savages for a time.

Champlain, from what he had learned from the five or six Carantouannais who had escaped from the attack of the Senecas while acting as guides to Brulé, expected the latter would soon return to the Huron country; and he left word, it seems, before his departure for the St. Lawrence, for his interpreter to continue his explorations — this time to the northward and northwestward of the Hurons; as there were rumors of wars between various tribes in those regions, which, should reports be verified, would interfere with the yearly visit of the savages to the French settlements to barter their furs.[2] But Brulé was content to rest for a season from his severe work of exploration to recuperate after so much suffering. Finally,

John Gilmary Shea, in *The Pennsylvania Magazine of History and Biography*, vol. II, p. 108. It is seldom that Mr. Shea, when it comes to a matter of translation from the French, is in error; but that Brulé fell in with a few Iroquois *going to the fields* is not in accordance with Champlain's account as given him by Brulé.

[1] Champlain speaks of them as "the Atinouaentans," using the term as synonymous with the later one — "the Hurons": "He [Brulé] went to the country and village of the Atinouaentans, where I had already been." The village was, probably, Toanché.

[2] Such is the only meaning we can give to Champlain's words, which, although vague, are, in the light of future events, most probable. He says (the italicising is mine): "And if Brulé had gone further on to explore these regions *as I had directed him to do*, it would not have been a mere rumor that they were preparing war with one another." (Champlain is speaking, of course, in 1618.)

without undertaking other researches, after remaining with the Hurons for many months, he concluded first to visit the settlements of his countrymen before again seeking to explore new and distant countries — before again making the acquaintance of strange tribes and risking his life among them. So, in the summer of 1618 (after eight years of continuous service in the wilderness),[1] joining his savage friends, who were ready to start upon their yearly visit to the French upon the St. Lawrence, Brulé, journeying by way of the Georgian bay of Lake Huron — boating for ten days along its northern shore to the mouth of French river — ascending that stream — crossing Lake Nipissing — and floating down the Ottawa — finally, on July 7th, greeted Champlain at Three Rivers, to recount to him, after almost a three years' absence since parting with him in the Huron country, the story of what he had seen of distant regions and of what he had suffered in his journeyings.[2]

Brulé, at his interview with Champlain, was

[1] See Appendix, Note XVI.

[2] The recital of Brulé of his discoveries, as given to Champlain upon his (Brulé's) return to the St. Lawrence, is printed in Champlain's *Voyages* of 1619. It is also to be found in the edition of 1627, but is omitted in the condensed edition of 1632. The probable reason for this omission will hereafter be given.

(See, in connection with Brulé's arrival at Three Rivers, the Appendix to our Narrative, Note XVI.)

Parkman suggests (*Pioneers of France in the New World*, p. 379*n*), that, as before stated, Brulé's name may possibly allude to the fiery ordeal through which he passed when in the hands of the Iroquois; but the way Champlain mentions him upon first seeing him after his return ("a man named Brulé") certainly makes this idea wholly improbable.

requested by the latter to continue his work among the savages. The propriety of his attempting other explorations was urged upon him; and the courageous woodman promised to make the attempt and then to conduct his patron to the region visited by him, that he himself might obtain fuller and more particular knowledge of ulterior countries.[1]

After Champlain had given his interpreter information as to his intention of soon sailing again for France (he had made a voyage thither the year before), and had assured him that, upon his coming back with more abundant means, he would be rewarded for what he had already accomplished,— Brulé took his leave to go again to the wilderness upon the return of the Indians to their homes. He was particularly requested by Champlain to tarry with the savages until the next year (1619), when his patron would go to him (with a good number of men), both to pay him for his labors, and to assist his friends — the Indians — in their wars, as in the past.[2] Champlain, however, never again ascended the Ottawa. "His forest rovings were over. The fire that had flashed the keen flame of daring adventure must now be subdued to the duller use of practical labor. To battle with savages and the elements was doubtless more congenial with his

[1] As has been previously stated, it is an inference of the writer of this narrative that Champlain desired Brulé to prosecute further discoveries by going to the northward and northwestward of the Hurons and had left word for him to do so, with the Hurons. Why it is probable this direction was given will presently appear.

[2] See Appendix, Note XVII, as to the reliability of Brulé's narrative.

nature than to nurse a puny colony into growth and strength; yet to each task he gave himself with the same strong devotion."[1] But Brulé had little to win him away from the life he had so long been living.[2]

---

[1] Parkman: *Pioneers of France in the New World*, p. 387. When Champlain visited the St. Lawrence in 1617, he expected to join with the savages in another expedition, but was disappointed; and the next year upon his return from France he satisfactorily explained to the savages why he failed. A Canadian historian, in speaking of this explanation by Champlain, says: "Champlain [in 1618] proceeded to Three Rivers; a great many Indians were present. They received him with their old respect and affection, and asked for his help in their wars. Champlain replied that he had not changed his feelings on the subject. He reminded them *how they had failed to attend with the requisite number of men, in the attack on the Seneca village; and that, consequently, he and his force had been compelled to retreat without effecting any good result* [the italicising is mine]."— Kingsford's *History of Canada*, vol. I, p. 56.

It will be seen that Mr. Kingsford, in this, makes Champlain speak to the assembled Indians at Three Rivers as though they were (at least some of them) Carantouannais, reminding them of their failure to assist him in the attack in 1615, on the Iroquois fort, which he speaks of as the Seneca (instead of Onondaga) village. Of course, this is a double error.

[2] "If I understand well the text of Champlain, Brulé roved in several countries until the spring of 1618, when he returned to Georgian Bay and from there joined the Hurons who were going to trade at Three Rivers. They arrived at that station in July, and Champlain noted down the observations of his interpreter with much delight. Brulé went back to Lake Huron without delay."— *Sulte*.

CHAPTER VIII.

BRULÉ DISCOVERS LAKE SUPERIOR.— HE VISITS THE NEUTRAL NATION.— RETURNS TO QUEBEC.— THE HUNDRED ASSOCIATES.— CAPTURE OF QUEBEC BY THE ENGLISH.— LAST JOURNEY OF BRULÉ TO THE HURONS.

In requesting Brulé to return to the savages, as Champlain did, in 1618, at Three Rivers, the latter was only acting in accordance with his policy of keeping suitable young men among the Indians, who, by becoming acquainted with remote regions and with the various languages of the natives thereof, might become of great assistance to him in his designs — particularly as relating to the fur trade — in New France.[1] As he intended to revisit the country bordering on Lake Huron, he urged Brulé at once to proceed on his tour of exploration to the northward. It is therefore to be presumed that the latter, on reaching the Georgian bay, turned his face in that direction, proceeding probably as far as the nation of the Beaver, living on the shores of what is now known as the North Channel.[2] After remaining there dur-

---

[1] Of all these young men, no one became, perhaps, so noted as John Nicolet (see *History of the Discovery of the Northwest, by John Nicolet, in* 1634, passim).

[2] If there were no other evidence to substantiate the fact of Brulé being sent to the northward, and northwestward — that is, to the nations living along the shores of the Georgian bay, and the North Channel,— what Champlain himself says is sufficient; for he was to go to the country where, it was rumored, the na-

ing the winter, and Champlain not making his appearance as he had been led to expect, Brulé was induced to return to the St. Lawrence, at least not later than in the summer of 1620, to find that the now acting governor of New France had but just returned from his native country.[1]

That the reports brought to Champlain by Brulé from the coast of the North Channel only served to increase the anxiety of the former for further intelligence of ulterior regions is evident. It was now apparently his principal wish that the interpreter should continue his journeyings until the mystery of the North Sea was solved. So, in 1621, Brulé again made his way to the Huron country, and started thence, with a companion (a Frenchman named Grenolle), for the north, from the town of Toanché.

Here, let us go back to Champlain's first visit to the St. Lawrence, in 1603. On June 18th of that year he set out from Tadoussac for the Lachine rapids, up the river. On the tenth of the next month (July), on his return-voyage, he questioned a young Algonquin about ulterior regions. The savages clearly pointed out the Ottawa river, Lake Nipissing, and, finally, Lake Huron — "a very large lake, some three hundred [French] leagues in length." Of course, this was an exaggeration. Proceeding northward some hundred leagues in this lake, the Indian said, a

tions were at war with each other. Surely this could not have been the case to the southward; as the Tobacco nation, the Cheveux Relevés and the Neutrals were not "at war with each other."

[1] Champlain became acting governor in 1619.

very large island (Great Manitoulin) would be reached. Another hundred leagues would bring one to the end of the lake (the distances again being overestimated), when rapids about a league wide (Sault Ste. Marie) could be seen, "where a very large mass of water" falls into Lake Huron. When these rapids are passed "one sees no more land on either side, but only a sea [Lake Superior] so large that they have never seen the end of it, nor heard that any one has." This was the first knowledge that was gained (and very imperfect it was) of the existence of Lake Superior by any white man. As to its waters being salt, the conclusion of Champlain was arrived at from erroneous information, of course, doubtless promoted by his eagerness to reach a northern ocean.[1]

Champlain inquired, at the same time, as to whether they had any knowledge of any mines.

[1] This record given by Champlain in the year 1603, concerning a great lake (or "sea," as he understood it) beyond Lake Huron, was the first account, really, ever published referring evidently to Lake Superior. Cartier, in his *Bref Récit*, printed in 1545, gives the particulars of the St. Lawrence flowing through several great lakes, as he was informed by the savages, the farthest of which was like a vast sea; but it is not certain whether Lake Superior or Lake Huron is referred to in this account; probably the last mentioned. Some have supposed that he even heard of the Mississippi:

"From them [the natives of Hochelaga], Cartier learned that it would take three months to sail in their canoes up the course of the majestic river [the St. Lawrence], which flowed beneath them, and that it ran through several great lakes, the farthest one of which was like a vast sea. Beyond this lake was another large river (the Mississippi), which pursued a southerly course through a region free from ice and snow."— MacMullen's *History of Canada*, p. 6. But that author draws largely on his imagination in thus identifying the Mississippi as the river referred to by Cartier.

They told him that the Hurons (who came to trade with the Algonquins for articles the latter had purchased from French vessels in the St. Lawrence) said that toward the north from their country was a mine of pure copper, some bracelets made from which they showed Champlain, they having obtained them from the Hurons. This information was the first obtained by any white man of the existence of the North Channel or of the Lake Superior copper-mines, except that, as already shown, Cartier, in 1535, learned that copper was brought from the Saguenay country,— an indefinite region to the northward and westward, including, however, that of Lake Superior.[1]

In 1610, Champlain, in going up the St. Lawrence to meet the savages at the island off the mouth of the Iroquois river, was met by a canoe containing two Indians—one a Montagnais, the other an Algonquin. The latter (a chief) drew from a sack a piece of copper a foot in length, which he gave to Champlain. It was very handsome and quite pure. He gave the Frenchman to

[1] When Cartier moved up the St. Lawrence in 1535, the savages pointed out the region of the Saguenay—an exceedingly indefinite one, stretching away without any fixed limits, to the north and to the west—which they said was inhabited; and thence came some red copper which they had, called by them "caignetdaze." As this red copper (*cyure rouge*) doubtless came from the copper mines of Lake Superior, it is in this information (very slight, it is true) that the first glimpse is caught of the Northwest. On his return down the river, Cartier saw "a great knife" made of this "red copper," in possession of some Montagnais, the latter presenting it to a chief of theirs, who was with Cartier,—having been captured by the latter [see Cartier's *Brief Récit* (D'Avezac Ed.), pp. 9, 34, 44, cited by the Rev. E. F. Slafter, in the *Prince Society Publications of Champlain's "Voyages,"* vol. II, p. 237*n*].

understand that there were large quantities where he had taken this, which was on the bank of a river, near a great lake. He said that they gathered it in lumps, and, having melted it, spread it in sheets, smoothing it with stones. Champlain says he was very glad of the present, although of small value. It was really, there seems no doubt, the second time he had received knowledge (although, of course, vaguely communicated) of the Lake Superior copper mines, and indeed of the great lake itself. However, the latter he would fain believe was a northern ocean. And it was several years before he was fully undeceived — before he fully realized that the boundless water, that is, boundless to the eyes of the savages as they looked to the northward and westward over its surface, was only a "Grand Lac." And it is just here that it is proper to show how and when he came to a full realization of the magnitude of this, the greatest lake on the globe.

There were three motives inducing Brulé, according to the declaration of Champlain, to remain in the wilderness among the Indians: (1) to pass his time; (2) to see the country; and (3) to learn the language of the savages and their mode of life. But all these came originally from the promptings of Champlain himself, as we have shown, who, it may be premised, did not fail for sixteen or seventeen years to urge them, with also another and particular object, that of persuading the Indians to go yearly to trade with the French upon the St. Lawrence.

It would indeed be strange if Champlain sent Brulé on a journey along the north coast, from the mouth of French river on Georgian bay, without having first given him all the information he had previously obtained of the country he was to visit and of the savages he was to meet;[1] particularly would he be told of the probable existence of mines of copper and of the great lake, or, rather, of an ocean — the "North Sea" of Champlain's imagination.

Not only Champlain but Brulé and Grenolle themselves must have heard much of the region from the Algonquins and Hurons, and of the Indians who lived there, for the latter had long traded with the former. These northern savages were known to be at war not only among themselves, but with other nations; and Brulé was to be a messenger of peace wherever he went, to the end that all might be induced to go down to the yearly trade upon the St. Lawrence.

But let us now follow the adventurous Frenchmen in their voyage to the northward. It seems certain that all the Indians visited were of Algonquin lineage; but where they lived and what were their names can only be gleaned from what is recorded of them a few years subsequent to this journey of Brulé and his companion. Three nations occupied the shores of the Georgian bay south of the

---

[1] But Champlain had gathered little from the Indians — very little even from the Hurons in his sojourn with them in 1615-'16 — as to the savage nations beyond their great lake ("Mer Douce," i. e., Lake Huron), except that prisoners taken from the more distant ones "said that still farther on towards the setting sun there was a people who had light-colored hair and looked like the French."— (See Winsor's *Cartier to Frontenac*, p. 120; *Champlain's "Voyages" — Prince Society Publications*, vol. III, p. 158, 159.)

mouth of French river.[1] Passing this stream going northward, Brulé probably sighted the Manitoulin islands stretching from east to west along the north shores of Lake Huron, and consisting chiefly of what is now known as the Great Manitoulin (or Sacred Isle), Little Manitoulin (or Cockburn), and Drummond. The island first mentioned is eighty miles long by twenty broad — the same that Champlain, as has been shown, gained some knowledge of from Indian report, in 1603. Northward of these islands were the hunting-grounds of that nation of savages known as Beavers, living upon the shores of the North Channel, as already related, though their ancient seat was the islands before described. That the two white men visited these Indians there can be no doubt. Farther on, but still upon the margin of the Huron lake, was found another nation — the Oumisagai.[2]

That Brulé and his companion went upon this journey is not at all a matter of conjecture as is the first visit of the former to the Beaver nation; for Sagard says:

"At about eighty or a hundred [French] leagues from the Hurons, there is a mine of red copper, from which the interpreter, Brulé, showed me a large ingot when he came back from a journey he made to a neighboring nation with a man named

[1] These were the Ouasouarim, the Outchougai, and the Atchiligoüan.

[2] Consult, as to the various nations inhabiting the shores of the Georgian bay, and the coast of the North Channel (as at present known), at about this period or a little later, the *History of the Discovery of the Northwest*, by *John Nicolet, in* 1634, pp. 50, 51.

Grenolle."[1] Sagard also confirms, in another mention of Grenolle, what he says as to the latter's visit, stating that it was for the purposes of trade:

"One of our Frenchmen named Crenole [Grenolle] having been to trade on the north coast, among a nation living about one hundred leagues from the Hurons, which nation was working in a copper mine, told us when he came back, of having seen among them several girls who had the ends of their noses cut off (following the custom of the country), for having committed offenses against chastity."[2]

We are left in the dark as to what savages were found by Brulé and Grenolle on the north shore, "working in a copper mine." That they were either the Beavers or the Oumisagai, already mentioned, is certain. How long the two tarried in that region is also unknown. Did they proceed onward to the mouth of the St. Mary river and up that stream to the rapids? It is reasonably certain they did. So it was that the "Sault de Ste. Marie" (rapids or falls of the St. Mary) was for the first time seen by white men, although, as already explained, they had been heard of by Champlain nearly twenty years previous.

Once at the falls, and Brulé and his companion

---

[1] *Histoire du Canada* (Paris Reprint, 1866), p. 716. (See Appendix to our Narrative, Note XXII [f].) Copper, in its native state, is found at various points on the coast of the North Channel, or, as we may say, on the "North Coast."

[2] See Note XXII [a], in Appendix. In the *History of the Discovery of the Northwest, by John Nicolet*, p. 49, the statement is made, in effect, that Nicolet, in 1634, was the first white man to explore the northern coast of Lake Huron (or Georgian bay, as now known); but this is error.

had reached the principal village of a savage nation afterwards designated the "People of the Falls,"—called by the French, "Sauteurs." They were the ancestors of the modern Otchipwes (misnamed Ojibwas), now generally known as Chippewas.[1]

Brulé would certainly not be content to terminate his journey at the falls, but would press onward until his eyes were gladdened by a view of the greatest body of fresh water on the globe — now the well-known Lake Superior.

"The interpreter, Brulé," says Sagard, "assured us that beyond the Freshwater Sea [Lake Huron] there was another very large lake which empties into it by a waterfall, which has been called 'Saut de Gaston' [Gaston Falls], of a width of almost two leagues; which lake and the Freshwater Sea have almost thirty days' journey by canoe in length, according to the account of the savages; but, according to the interpreter's [Brulé's] account, they are four hundred [French] leagues in length."[2]

No white man before Brulé had stood upon the shores of Lake Superior. It was the "North Sea" of Champlain's fondest hopes; but, alas, its waters were fresh. It could not, therefore, lead

[1] It is not certain on which side of the river was located, at this date, the principal village of the Chippewas.

[2] Sagard — *Histoire du Canada* (Paris Reprint, 1866), p. 589. (See Appendix to our Narrative, Note XXII [e].) As to the falls having been, soon after Brulé's visit, known as the "Sault de Gaston," see also Index to Champlain's map of 1632. Winsor, in *Cartier to Frontenac*, p. 144, mentions who it was that the name was intended to commemorate. (Consult, further, as to the evidence of Brulé's discovery of Lake Superior, Appendix to our Narrative, Note XVIII.)

directly to China. To it was given no particular name — it was sufficient to designate it, at first, as the "Great Lake." It is probable that the adventurers paddled their canoe along its northern shore until they came to its head, entering the mouth of the St. Louis river near where now are the cities of Superior and Duluth. In returning, it is conjectured they visited Isle Royale.[1] Brulé reached Quebec July 2nd, 1623, visiting, on the twenty-third, three hundred Indians (Hurons) at Chaudière (now the city of Ottawa), coming down the river to trade. The same summer he went back to the Huron country.

But Brulé, the next year (1624), again returned to the St. Lawrence. On this trip he journeyed with a party of Hurons, they having nine loaded canoes. They were on their way down to barter their furs with the French at Quebec. Most of the distance they were accompanied by the Friar Sagard in a canoe in which were only himself and attendants. The good friar frequently mentions "the Interpreter Brulé" (as he always calls him), in recording incidents of the journey.

The Indians showed him (Sagard) several rocks on the road to Quebec, and among others they pointed out one which had a deep cavern, very difficult of access. They wished to persuade him into believing absolutely with them that this rock had formerly been a man; and that upon an occasion of the latter having his hands and arms raised high, he had been transformed into stone and in course of time became the wonderful rock before them.

[1] See Appendix, Note XVIII.

This rock, Sagard declares, the savages hold in veneration and offered to it tobacco in passing before it in their canoes — "not every time," he says, "but when they are doubtful of their voyage being successful; and when offering this tobacco, which they throw into the water against the rock itself, they say to it: 'Hear! Take courage and give us a good voyage,' — with some other words which I do not understand; and the Interpreter Brulé .... told us (to our confusion) that he once made a similar offering with them (for which we rebuked him severely), and that his voyage was made more profitable to him than any others which he had ever made in all these regions."[1]

After reaching the St. Lawrence and while at the Saut S. Louis (Lachine rapids), the friar records that he had, upon his arrival there, a bad sleeping place, and that he was no better off the following night, because of a heavy rain. At "Cape Victory" he overtook "the Interpreter Brulé," who had arrived there with his Hurons two days before. From him he learned that some Montagnais and Algonquins had forbidden them to pass further down the river. It was a scheme on the part of the Indians last mentioned to blackmail the strangers. The latter at first determined to resist. This, Sagard declares, was a dangerous

---

[1] See Appendix, Note XXII [d]. It appears from the above that Brulé, previous to this visit to the Hurons, had, occasionally, while engaged in acquiring different Indian languages or in exploration and discovery, employed some of his time in trafficking with the savages, — probably having with him trinkets of no great value which he exchanged for furs.

resolve, particularly to Brulé, whose bag of tobacco the Montagnais and Algonquins especially coveted.

But the Montagnais and Algonquins hesitated before offering force to the Huron party. Finally, they assured them they had just received some valuable presents from a tribe who were mortal enemies of the Hurons, on condition that they would send them word when the latter made their appearance — to the end that they might come and put them all to death, and that they would soon arrive. This so terrified Brulé and his party that they made the Montagnais and Algonquins a liberal donation of nets, tobacco, flour and other things, and were allowed to pass on without further molestation; but Sagard refused to make them any gifts; and early the next morning, while all were asleep, he quietly dropped his canoe into the river and was soon beyond reach of the wily savages.[1]

A change was now (1625) at hand in the affairs of New France. Two Huguenots, William and Emery de Caen, had taken the place of the old company of St. Malo and Rouen, but were afterward compelled to share their monopoly with them. Fresh troubles were thus introduced into the infant colony, not only in secular matters but in religious affairs. The Récollets had previously established five missions, extending from Acadia to the borders of Lake Huron. Now, three Jesuits — among their number John de Brébeuf — arrived in the colony, and began their spiritual labors.

The year 1625 found Brulé again among the Hurons. When, nine years before, Champlain visited

[1] Appendix, Note XXII [h].

the Cheveux Relevés, he was farther west from the St. Lawrence than any other white man had been — farther, indeed, than was his adventurous interpreter when at the head of Lake Ontario the previous fall; but now Brulé was ready to start on an exploring tour which would take him beyond the western limits reached by his patron, but in a direction southwesterly from the Hurons. It was to the villages of the Neutrals he was going, which had never been visited by a white man. He must have previously obtained some interesting particulars from the Hurons concerning these savages, as there was frequent intercourse between the two nations. To most of them the sight of Brulé would be a great surprise; a few, however, had doubtless already seen him in some one of the Huron towns.

The hunting grounds of the Neutral nation extended from a day's journey west of the territory of the Senecas onward nearly to the eastern shores of Lake Huron. The real name of these savages was Attiwandaron; they had twenty-eight towns and several little hamlets of seven or eight cabins each. Their villages were built after the manner of those of the Hurons; and their language was the same, radically, as the latter.

There are no particulars extant of Brulé's journey to the Neutrals. That he explored the larger portion of their country lying to the westward of the Niagara is evident. He would have no curiosity, however, to see that river, as he had already been there on his way to and from Carantouan.

Brulé was delighted with the country of the Attiwandarons. He, it is believed, remained there until the next spring, and then returned to the St. Lawrence.

In the summer of 1626, Fathers Brébeuf and De Noue, Jesuits, with Joseph de la Roche Daillon, a Franciscan priest, as escort, started for the Huron country, which they reached after a most laborious journey of three weeks. "Though far away," wrote the latter in July of the next year, from Toanché, to a friend in Paris, "it is still permitted us to visit our friends by missions which render the absent present. Our Indians were amazed at it, seeing us often write to our Fathers at a distance, and that by our letters they learn our ideas and what the [same] Indians had done at our residence. After having made some stay in our Canada convent, and communicated with our Fathers and the [Reverend] Jesuit Fathers, I was compelled by a religious affection to visit the sedentary nations, whom we call Hurons; and with me [went] the Rev. Fathers Brébeuf and De Noue, Jesuits,— having arrived there with all the hardships that any one may imagine, by reason of the wretched way."

"Some time afterwards," continues Daillon, "I received a letter from our Reverend Father, Joseph le Caron, by which he encouraged me to pass on to a nation we call 'Neutral,' of which the interpreter Brulé told wonders. Encouraged, then, by so good a Father, and the grand account given me of these people [by Brulé], I started for their country, setting out from the Hurons with this design, October 18th, 1626, with men called Grenolle and Lavalée, Frenchmen by birth. Passing the Petun [Tobacco] nation, I . . . arrived at the first village [of the Neutrals], where we were well received, thanks to our Lord, and then at four other villages, which envied each other in bringing us food." . . .

"After all this cordial welcome," are the further words of the Rev. Father, "our Frenchmen [Grenolle and Lavalée] returned and I remained, the happiest man in the world, hoping to do something there to advance God's glory, or at least to discover . . . . the mouth of the river of the Hiroquois [Niagara], in order to bring them [the Neutrals] to trade [with the French, by way of Lake Ontario]."

But there are other particulars recorded in this letter of the Franciscan friar of the greatest importance, as verifying the story told him by Brulé. Was the "grand account" of the interpreter true? Did he exaggerate in his recital of the "wonders" of that region? Let us see. Here is the narration of Daillon: "The country of this Neutral nation is incomparably larger, more beautiful, and better than any other of all these countries. There is an incredible number of stags, great abundance of moose, or elk, beaver, wildcats, and black squirrels . . . . a great quantity of wild geese, turkeys, cranes, and other animals, which are there all winter. . . . The rivers furnish much excellent fish; the earth gives good grain, more than is needed. They have squashes, beans, and other vegetables in abundance."[1]

In the spring of 1627, a report having spread among the Hurons that Daillon had been killed,

[1] See Very Rev. W. R. Harris's translation of Daillon's letter, in *Early Missions in Western Canada*, pp. 50–55.

Fathers Brébeuf and De Noue sent Grenolle to the Neutrals to learn whether it was true or not. The latter soon returned with Daillon to Toanché.[1]

When the year 1627 was reached, the settlement at Quebec had a population of about one hundred persons — men, women and children. The chief trading stations upon the St. Lawrence were Quebec, Three Rivers, the Rapids of St. Louis, and Tadoussac.[2]

In the year last mentioned, the destinies of France were held by Cardinal Richelieu as in the hollow of his hand. He had constituted himself grand master and superintendent of navigation and commerce. By him the privileges of the Caens were annulled, and a company formed, consisting of a hundred associates, called the Company of New France. At its head was Richelieu himself. Louis the Thirteenth made over to this company forever the fort and settlement at Quebec, and all the territory of New France, including Florida. To them was given power to appoint judges, build fortresses, cast cannon, confer titles, and concede lands. They were to govern in peace and in war. Their monopoly of the fur trade was made perpetual; while that of all other commerce within the

---

[1] Harris, loc. cit. (See, also, Appendix to our Narrative, Note XIX.) In Garneau's *Canada* (Bell's translation, vol. I, p. 95), it is said four Récollets arrived in Canada in 1615; that they visited the Hurons along with Champlain; and that one of them the next year went to the Neutral nation. There are two prominent errors in this recital: only one of the friars (Le Caron) went to the Hurons; and the Neutrals were not visited the next year at all; it was the Tobacco nation.

[2] *History of the Discovery of the Northwest, by John Nicolet, in 1634,* pp. 20, 21.

limits of their government was limited to fifteen years, except that the whale-fishery and cod-fishery were to remain open to all. They could take whatever steps they might think expedient or proper for the protection of the colony and the fostering of trade. It will thus be seen that the Hundred Associates had conferred upon them almost sovereign power. For fifteen years their commerce was not to be troubled with duties or imposts. Partners, whether nobles, officers, or ecclesiastics, might engage in commercial pursuits without derogating from the privileges of their order. To all these benefits the king added a donation of two ships of war. Of this powerful association, Champlain was one of the members.

In return for these privileges conferred, behold how little these hundred partners were compelled to perform. They engaged to convoy to New France, during 1628, two or three hundred men of all trades, and before the year 1643 to increase the number to four thousand persons of both sexes; to supply all their settlers with lodging, food, clothing, and farm implements, for three years; then they would allow them sufficient land to support themselves, cleared to a certain extent; and would also furnish them the grain necessary for sowing it; stipulating, also, that the emigrants should be native Frenchmen and Roman Catholics, and none others; and, finally, agreeing to settle three priests in each settlement, whom they were bound to provide with every article necessary for their personal comfort, and to defray the expenses of their ministerial labors for fifteen years. After the expiration of that time, cleared lands were to be granted by the company to the clergy for maintaining the Roman Catholic Church in New France. It was thus that the Hundred Associates became proprietors of the whole country claimed by France, from Florida to the Arctic Circle; from Newfoundland to the sources of the St. Lawrence and its tributaries. Meanwhile, the fur trade had brought a considerable knowledge of the Ottawa, and of the country of the Hurons, to the French upon the St. Lawrence, through the yearly visits of the savages from those distant parts and the journeyings of the fur trader in quest of peltry.[1]

In April, 1628, the first vessel of the Hundred Associates sailed from France with colonists and supplies, bound for the St. Lawrence. Four of these vessels were armed. Everything seemed propitious for a speedy arrival at Quebec, where the inhabitants were sorely pressed for food; but a storm, which had for some time been brewing in Europe, broke in fury upon New France. The imprudent zeal of the Catholics in England, and the persecution of the Huguenots in France, aroused the English, who determined to conquer the French possessions in North America, if possible; and, to that end, they sent out David Kirk,[2] with an armed squadron, to attack the settlements in Canada. The fleet reached the harbor of Tadoussac before the arrival of the vessels of the Company of New France. Kirk sent a demand for the surrender of Quebec, but Champlain determined to defend the place; at least, he resolved to

---

[1] Id., pp. 21–23.

[2] Synonyms: Kirke, Kirtk, Kyrck, Kertk, Kerk, Ker, Quer, Querch, Quercq.

make a show of defense; and the English commander thought best not to attack such a formidable looking position. All the supplies sent by the Hundred Associates to the St. Lawrence were captured or sunk.

Although in the summer of 1627 Brulé had again journeyed to the Hurons, he could not have remained with them later than the next year, as 1628 finds him again on the St. Lawrence.

Quebec, as we have just seen, had been summoned to surrender, but had not yet capitulated to the English. There was great distress there. "Seven ounces of pounded pease were now the daily food of each; and, at the end of May [1629], even this failed. Men, women and children betook themselves to the woods, gathering acorns and grubbing up roots. . . . Some joined the Hurons or the Algonquins; some wandered towards the Abenakis of Maine; some descended in a boat to Gaspé, trusting to meet a French fishing-vessel. There was scarcely one who would not have hailed the English as deliverers."[1]

Kirk's vessels which, in 1628, had ascended the St. Lawrence had returned to France after capturing the supply-vessels of the Hundred Associates; but, in 1629, he returned with a squadron. Four Frenchmen went over to the English, one of whom was Brulé. The brothers of the Admiral — Lewis and Thomas — would again ask Champlain to surrender, but this time from a point nearer Quebec than Tadoussac. Three English ships were to be sent up to enforce the demand. A pilot was nec-

[1] Parkman's *Pioneers of France in the New World*, pp. 405, 406.

essary, and Brulé acted as such. Capitulation followed.[1]

"Thirteen of the French colonists, looking perhaps on the change as a deliverance, as Charlevoix intimates, were induced to live under the English rule. Of these, there were seven who were of importance to the victors, because of their woodcraft and experience with the Indians." Brulé was severely censured afterwards for having aided the English vessels to ascend to Quebec, thereby helping materially to the surrender of the place; but he knew that capitulation would save the occupants from starvation.[2]

After most of its inhabitants had dispersed in the forests for food, Quebec surrendered. England thus gained her first supremacy upon the great river of Canada.

The terms of the capitulation were that the French were to be conveyed to their own country; and each soldier was allowed to take with him furs to the value of twenty crowns.[3] As some had lately returned from the Hurons with peltry of no small value, their loss was considerable. The French prisoners, including Champlain, were conveyed across the ocean by Kirk, but their arrival in England was after a treaty of peace had been

---

[1] Charlevoix says (see Shea's translation, vol. II, p. 50): "Kertk [Kirk] then landed at Quebec and took possession of the fort, then of the warehouse, the keys of which he committed to one Le Baillif, of Amiens, who had gone over to the enemy with three other Frenchmen,—Stephen Brulé, of Champigny; Nicholas Marsolet, of Rouen; and Peter Raye, of Paris."

[2] See Appendix, Note XX.

[3] For the terms of the treaty in full, see Smith's *Canada*, vol. I, p. 22.

CAPTURE OF QUEBEC BY THE ENGLISH, 1629.
[Fac-simile of the engraving in Hennepin's *New Discovery*, 1698, p. 161.]
By courtesy of Houghton, Mifflin & Company.

signed between the two powers. The result was the restoration of New France to the French crown; and on July 5th, 1632, Émery de Caen cast anchor at Quebec to reclaim the country.[1] Of course, Brulé did not return with the French prisoners to France when Quebec surrendered, but again journeyed to the Hurons sometime before the arrival of De Caen.[2] He was accompanied by Amantacha, a native Huron,[3] who, in 1626 (then a mere lad), was sent to France by the missionaries, where he was baptized. Having been instructed there by the Jesuits, he returned to Canada before the capture of Quebec by the English,— subsequent to which event he entered into their service as interpreter.

[1] *History of the Discovery of the Northwest by John Nicolet, in* 1634, pp. 23, 24. As to affairs on the St. Lawrence, from 1617 to 1633, see, of works in English, Parkman's *Pioneers of France in the New World*, pp. 390-412; Warburton's *Conquest of Canada*, vol. I, pp. 89-95; Slafter, in *Memoir of Champlain* — vol. I, of the *Prince Society Publications of Champlain's "Voyages,"* pp. 143-178; same, in "Champlain" —Winsor's *Narrative and Critical History of America*, vol. IV, pp. 126-129; also Winsor's *Cartier to Frontenac*, pp. 121-146.

[2] On March 29th, 1632, by the terms of the treaty, Canada was ceded by England to France. De Caen took possession of Quebec, July 13th, of that year.

[3] Known among the French as "Louis de Sainte Foi."

CHAPTER IX.

BRULÉ KILLED AND EATEN BY HURONS.—HIS DEATH SOON KNOWN ABROAD.—THE FEAR OF THE SAVAGES BECAUSE OF THEIR DEED.

Once again among the Hurons, and Brulé, it seems, gave himself wholly to a savage life; but his Indian friends could not forget he was a white man.[1] At Toanché,[2] in 1632 (that this was the year it is now sufficiently established), he was barbarously and treacherously murdered — clubbed to death — by those in whom he had always placed the utmost confidence as his faithful protectors. What cause he had given them — whether fancied or real — for their bloodthirsty and most cruel act is unknown. But their savageness did not stop with his death. In their wild and horrible ferocity to take revenge on their victim, they feasted upon his lifeless remains."[3]

[1] "When Canada was taken by Kirk, Brulé went over to the English, but finally returned to the Huron country, and became a thorough Indian."— John Gilmary Shea, in *The Pennsylvania Magazine of History and Biography*, vol. II, p. 108.

[2] This Huron village — chief town of the Bear clan, or tribe — seems to have been the favorite dwelling place of Brulé while in the Huron country. Its exact site is not known. Consult, in this connection, Thwaites' *Jesuit Relations and Allied Documents*, vol. V, p. 293.

[3] Says Shea: "At last he [Brulé] gave offense to his new countrymen, and they not only killed, but ate him." (*The Pennsylvania Magazine of History and Biography*, vol. II, p. 108.) See, as to the cannibalism of the Hurons, Appendix to our Narrative, Note XXI.

"Brulé," says Sagard, "was killed and then eaten by the Hurons, whom he had so long served as interpreter; and all for the hatred which they bore him; but I do not know what offense he committed against them. There were many years that he was living among them, following the customs of the country and serving as interpreter; and all that he received as his reward was a painful death — a nefarious and unhappy end. I pray God to be merciful toward him, if it please Him, and to have pity on his soul."[1]

The killing of Brulé was soon known to all the surrounding nations. The news was by no means disagreeable to those tribes having, as had the Hurons, traffic relations with the French. It was their desire, if not their expectation, that reprisals would be the result and, possibly, war. In such an event, there would be less competition and their own furs would command better prices upon the St. Lawrence.

It was in the year 1633 that Champlain was again clothed with authority in Canada. English domination had already ceased, and with his commission renewed he resumed, on the twenty-third of May, command at Quebec in behalf of the Hundred Associates. Scarcely two months elapsed when he received good news from up the Ottawa. There would soon arrive a large number of Hu-

---

[1] *Histoire du Canada* (Paris Reprint, 1866), p. 430. (See Appendix to our Narrative, Note XXII [c].) Language so sympathetic would hardly have been used by that writer had he believed Brulé to have been a bad man. He knew him; and the prayer of the good friar would surely not have had much heart in it, had he held his memory in abhorrence because of his going over to the English when Quebec fell into their hands.

rons having many canoe-loads of peltry for barter with the French traders. However, there soon came ill-tidings: thus far, only small parties had reached their destination, having each but few canoes. It seems that the Island Savages, that is, the "Nation de l'Isle" of the French — inhabitants of Alumettes Island — and the other Algonquins, living on the route from the Hurons to Quebec, had tried to dissuade these Indian traders from visiting Champlain, telling them the French would do them a bad turn on account of their killing Brulé and that an Algonquin of the Little Nation, having killed a Frenchman, had been taken prisoner and condemned to death; also, that the same would be done to some Hurons. Their design was to get all the merchandise from these Hurons at a very low price, in order afterwards to come themselves and trade it, either with the French or the English.

At this juncture, Amantacha, the Huron, was at Quebec. He was sent by Champlain to meet the Indians. He assured those of his tribe of the good feeling of the French toward them, declaring that they might put him to death if the French did not give them a warm welcome. As to Brulé, who had been murdered, Amantacha declared he was not looked upon as a Frenchman, because he had left his nation and gone over to the English. This proved to be a convincing argument to the savages — completely allaying their fears. On July 28th, Amantacha came back to Champlain; and the next day not less than five hundred Hurons, in about one hundred and forty canoes, all at once made their appearance and the most cordial greetings followed.

In 1634, the missionary Brébeuf, having again determined to start a mission among the Hurons, reached his old town of Toanché, where he had lived three years — from 1626 to 1629 — but it was now a desolation. Only a vestige of his little bark chapel was remaining; — the village had been burnt to the ground; its inhabitants had fled to a spot some distance away, where they had built a new town — all because they feared some terrible judgment would overtake them if they longer remained where Brulé was killed; they would, if possible, avert what was feared might be an awful punishment for their crime. Brébeuf found, as he believed, the very spot where "poor Brulé" died.[1]

But the removal from Toanché did not avail to secure immunity to the Indians of the place. A terrible pestilence devastated the land a considerable time after the event, and not a few of the savages were convinced it was because of their deed. A sister of the murdered Brulé was said to have been seen flying over the country, breathing death and destruction as she hastened onward. She was her brother's avenger; and nothing could stay her onward course. — So it was that the woman carried terror to the minds of the guilty Hurons, and the deadly pestilence could not be assuaged.

[1] Brébeuf, *Relation des Hurons*, 1635, pp. 28, 29: "I saw also the place where the poor Étienne Brulé had been barbarously and treacherously murdered." It is evident Brébeuf harbored no ill-will against Brulé. His language was very different from that of Champlain, given in the "Voyages" of 1632.

APPENDIX.

NOTE I.

CHAMPLAIN'S WORKS.

The "Voyages" of Champlain, which might with much propriety be termed his "Journals," were published at different times from 1603 to 1632. The first volume was printed in 1603 under the title *Des Sauvages*,* the next publication appeared in 1613, republished in 1615 and 1617; the next, in 1619 (reissued in 1620 and 1627); and the next and last—"a compendium of all his previous publications, with much additional matter"—in 1632 (reissued, it is said, in 1640).

The edition of 1632 comprises extended extracts from what Champlain had already published, and a continuation of the narrative to 1631. There is also published in the same volume a Treatise on Navigation, and a Catechism translated from the French by one of the Fathers into the language of the Montagnais.†

The complete works of Champlain in French are accessible to the reader in the volumes entitled:

"Œuvres de Champlain, publiées sous, le Patronage de l'Université Laval. Par l'Abbé C. H. Laverdière, M. A. Seconde Edition [the first Edition was burned]. 6 tomes, 4to. Québec: Imprimé au Séminaire par Geo. E. Desbarats, 1870."

In 1878, 1880 and 1882, an English translation of the "Voyages" of Champlain of 1604, of 1613 and 1619, was printed by the Prince Society, in three volumes, under the title of *Voyages of Samuel de Champlain. Translated from the French by Charles Pomeroy Otis, Ph.D. With Historical Illustrations and a*

---

*Translated, the title reads—"The Savages, or Voyage of Samuel de Champlain of Brouage, Made in New France in the year 1603."

†"The volume of 1632 contains what is not given in any of the previous publications of Champlain. That is, it extends his narrative over the period from 1620 to 1632. It likewise goes over the same ground that is covered not only by the volume of 1613, but also by the other still later publications of Champlain, up to 1620. It includes, moreover, a treatise on navigation. In the second place, it is an abridgment, and not a second edition in any proper sense."—Charles Pomeroy Otis, in vol. I, of *Champlain's "Voyages"* (*Publications of the Prince Society*), p. 219.

Memoir by the Rev. Edmund F. Slafter, A. M. The "Memoir" occupies the greater part of vol. I; and both the "Memoir" and the "Voyages" are learnedly annotated.

"His [Champlain's] books," says Parkman, "mark the man,— all for his theme and his purpose, nothing for himself. Crude in style, full of the superficial errors of carelessness, and haste, rarely diffuse, often brief to a fault, they bear on every page the palpable impress of truth [*Pioneers of France in the New World*, p. 420]." But it cannot be said, strictly speaking, that the edition of 1632 is one of "his books"— that is, in its entirety, as will now be seen.

"The most competent critics who have examined the edition of 1632 . . . including Laverdière, Margry, and Harrisse, agree that it bears internal evidence of having been compiled by a foreign hand, from the various editions previously published."— Marshall, in *The Magazine of American History*, vol. II, p. 472.

"Although the final edition of Champlain's narratives bears the date of 1632, there are some reasons to think that it was really issued the following year (1633), after Champlain had returned to Quebec. This book, in which several Paris publishers seem to have been conjointly interested, contains in the first part a condensation of his previous publications, and in the second a continuation of his experiences from 1620 to 1631. The last year's doings were apparently not written by Champlain himself. Indeed, it is manifest to more careful critics that the volume, including its map, failed to receive Champlain's personal supervision, and was prepared for the press by another hand."— Winsor: *Cartier to Frontenac*, pp. 139-141.

This edition (that of 1632), says Kingsford, in his *History of Canada*, was "an engine to influence opinion, so that Canada, restored to France, should be given over entirely to the Jesuits." * As to that author's criticisms on the concluding chapters, see vol. I, of his work just cited, p. 101*n*. (Compare, in this connection, Winsor: *Cartier to Frontenac*, pp. 141-144.)

NOTE II.

OF THE HURONS, ALGONQUINS, MONTAGNAIS AND IROQUOIS.

The first name given to the Hurons by Champlain was Ochastaiguins, or Ochateguins, after one of their chiefs named Ochateguin. They were nicknamed "Hurons" by the French, from

---

* Canada yielded to the English in 1629, as shown in our Narrative, but was "restored to France" in 1632.

their manner of wearing their hair: "*Quelle hures!* What boars' heads!" said they; and so they got to calling them "Hurons".—Charlevoix' *History of New France* (Shea's Translation), vol. II, p. 71. Champlain afterward called them "Attigouautans," but their true name was "Wendat" (or, as the French spelled it, "Ouendat").

The term "Algonquin," as used by Champlain, was given by him first to all those Indians not Hurons who came down the Ottawa. Afterwards, he restricted the name, applying it only to those who actually lived upon that river below the portage leading to Lake Nipissing. There never was an Algonquin (or Algonkin) nation; that is, one having that name as belonging distinctively to it, so called by themselves and other nations. Soon, however, the "Algonquins" of Champlain became the "Ottawas" of other writers (the name having many synonyms). Finally, "Algonquin" took on a broader signification, being applied only in a generic sense, to designate all those nations speaking languages radically similar (first to the Ottawas and then to others), wherever found.

The Montagnais — the "rabble of the woods" — occupied the St. Lawrence and northern water-courses to Hudson's bay. They were of a low type.

"The Montagnais or Montaignets had their great trading-post at Tadoussac, and roamed over a vast territory north and east of that point, and west of it as far as the mountains that separate the Saguenay and those of the Ottawa. The name was given to them by the French from this mountain range."—Slafter: *Prince Society Publications of Champlain's "Voyages,"* vol. II, p. 196*n*. There was no one nation, however, having properly "Montagnais" as its name.

The Iroquois (mention of whom is also made in Chapters III and IV of this narrative) were a formidable confederacy of five savage nations dwelling in fortified villages within limits now embraced by the State of New York. They spoke a language radically similar to the Hurons; but they were the deadly foes of the latter, and were at war also with the Montagnais and the Algonquins.

The name Iroquois was given these savages by the French. Charlevoix explains the meaning by referring it to the words used by those Indians whenever they came to the ending of an address, or speech, in their councils. But this is undoubtedly error, as the word is used by Champlain before any Frenchmen had ever been present at their meetings.

NOTE III.

EXCHANGE OF HOSTAGES—BRULÉ AND SAVIGNON.

"He [Champlain] joined their [the Indians'] camp near the mouth of the Richelieu River, and led them to an attack on an Iroquois barricade, which had been hastily constructed, not far up the river. The attack was so successful that not a hostile savage escaped.

"It was after this June onset, and while he was encamped with his allies on an island in Lake St. Peter, that he and they made a mutual exchange of hostages, in giving and taking a young man on each side. Champlain received the savage Savignon, whom he later took to France, and he gave them a young Frenchman,— there is reason to believe he is the same who later became known as Étienne Brulé."— Justin Winsor, in *Cartier to Frontenac*, pp. 99, 100.

That the young Frenchman was Brulé, is made certain by Champlain's own words spoken in 1618, when he says Brulé had then been living with the Indians eight years. (Note XVI, post.) He must have gone with them, then, in 1610, which, as just shown, was the year he left Champlain to go with the Indians; and it is evident no other white person in that year or previously had been sent among the savages.

A recent writer, after speaking of the capture of the Iroquois fort, or barricade, by Champlain and his Indian allies, June 19, 1610, alludes to Brulé, but only as a "young Frenchman"; he gives him no name: "When the celebration of the victory had been completed, the Indians departed to their distant abodes. Champlain, however, before their departure, very wisely entered into an agreement that they should receive for the winter a young Frenchman who was anxious to learn their language, and, in return, he was himself to take a young Huron, at their special request, to pass the winter in France. This judicious arrangement, in which Champlain was deeply interested and which he found some difficulty in accomplishing, promised an important future advantage in extending the knowledge of both parties, and in strengthening on the foundation of personal experience their mutual confidence and friendship."— Rev. E. F. Slafter, in vol. I (pp. 102, 103), of *Champlain's "Voyages"—Prince Society Publications*. Parkman (in *Pioneers of France in the New World*, p. 335n) seems not to have had a suspicion that Champlain's servant was Brulé: "The first white man to descend the rapids of St. Louis was a youth who had volunteered the previous summer [1610] to go with the Hurons to their country."

Again, he says (p. 339): "After his [Champlain's] second fight with the Iroquois, a young man of his company had boldly volunteered to join the Indians on their homeward journey and winter among them."

The following extracts, taken from the Ottawa *Evening Journal* of Jan. 12, 1889, are from an article by Mr. Benjamin Sulte, entitled "Annals of the Ottawa." Mr. Sulte clearly identifies Champlain's "young man" as Brulé:

"The French archives are replete with detailed information on the various expeditions of their people in the early days of this colony, but no precise note has been kept of the first attempts, if any, made to discover the valley of the Ottawa [river, Canada] before the years 1610–'13.

"I must mention the voyage of Samuel Champlain from Tadoussac to Montreal in 1603. At Tadoussac, he spoke to some Algonquins of the Ottawa, who had come there during their usual summer wanderings. Tessouat was the chief of that band, and his village was on the Allumette island. On their way down the St. Lawrence they had killed some Iroquois, which gave them an opportunity to celebrate their victory in the presence of Champlain, with a view to show him the valor of 'the noble red man.'

"A few weeks afterwards, Champlain visited the Island of Montreal, and enquired of the origin of the St. Lawrence River, but his report says nothing concerning the Ottawa except these two lines: 'There is a river going to the country of the Algonquins, who reside at a distance of some sixty leagues from the St. Lawrence.' The Island of Montreal was without inhabitants in 1603. According to some traditions, the Huron-Iroquois of the time of Cartier had been driven away by the Algonquins in the second half of the sixteenth century.

"When Champlain came back [from France] five years later (1608), he met at Quebec the son of an Algonquin chief called Iroquet. . . . Later on, Iroquet solicited Champlain to follow him in a campaign against the Iroquois. Consequently, by the end of June, 1609, they met near Lake St. Peter, and marched in the direction of the River Chambly and then to Lake Champlain, where they fought a battle. On the occasion, Iroquet was accompanied by a band of Indians under a chief named Ochatequin, great enemies of the Iroquois, and the same that Champlain had heard of in 1603, when the Algonquins described them as 'good Iroquois'. Hurons is their name in our History. They [the Hurons] lived on the south shore of Penetanguishene Bay, extending towards Lake Simcoe, as this bay and lake are now named, and spoke the same language as the Iroquois, who belonged to the same race but inhabited the south side of Lake Ontario, afterwards so-called, from what is now Buffalo to the present Albany.

"The Hurons came to Montreal and the Lower St. Lawrence through what is now termed French River, Lake Nipissing, River Matawan and the Ottawa. No doubt Champlain obtained from those people a good deal of information concering the west, and especially the Ottawa. He had already seen (in 1603) specimens of native copper taken, as stated by the Indians, from the vicinity of a large sea, which no doubt is Lake Superior.

"Now comes the expedition of Champlain from Quebec to Lake St. Peter, in 1610, marked by three important facts: a battle with the Iroquois, a large trade with the tribes of the Upper St. Lawrence and Upper Ottawa, and the departure of a young man who followed the Algonquins in their return home.—Who was this young man? . . . We will try to find out.

"Two-thirds of the men who had remained in Quebec the first autumn (1608) of the establishment of that post, died during the winter from the effects of a scorbutic disease. In the spring seven men only were living with Champlain himself. One of them was a young man named Étienne (Stephen, in English) Brulé, a native of Champigny, a small place near Paris. I believe he was the first white individual who saw the Ottawa Valley; this is how I explain it:

"The object of enlisting Brulé, Nicolet, Marsolet, Hertel, Marguerie and other grown-up boys for service in Canada from 1608 to 1620 was to educate them as interpreters. They all could read and write; some of them were even perfect scholars. In less than one year each of these young adventurers used to learn an Indian language, and sometimes they mastered two or three idioms after a very short period. . . .

"During the summer of 1610, Iroquet attended the trade business at Lake St. Peter. Champlain asked him to take a man with him in order to visit his country and report about it. The offer was accepted, provided an Indian would be chosen to embark for France for the same purpose. Savignon, who belonged to the Huron tribes, was selected to make the trip to Paris. Champlain recites on this ocasion: 'I had a young man who had already spent two winters at Quebec and who desired to go with the Algonquins to learn their language. I thought it well to send him in that direction because he could see the country, also the great lake (Huron), observe the rivers, the people, the mines and other rare things, so as to report truth about all this. He accepted the duty with pleasure.'

"No name is given. In all the narratives of Champlain, previous to this date [1610], we find no trace of any white man attempting to visit the Ottawa. This one must be considered the first explorer. But who was he? If you turn to Champlain's 'Journal,' during the summer of 1618, you will read that Étienne Brulé had been at that date eight years amongst the Indians. . . . Brulé, or the lad sent to Upper Canada by Champlain [in 1610], had at the same time an opportunity of observing the usages of the savages.

"When summer (1611) came bright again on the St. Lawrence, Champlain paddled his canoe from Quebec to Montreal and awaited for the arrival of his friends of the forest. Savignon accompanied him, and his impatience to see his relatives was so great that he started ahead to meet them but only went as far as Lake Two Mountains. . . . Listen to Champlain's report. 'On the 13th June, 1611, arrived two hundred Charioquois (Hurons) with Captains Ochateguin and Iroquet, also Tregouaroti, a brother of Savignon, and they brought back my young man [Brulé] who had mastered their language very well. Four of them assured me that they had seen the sea at a considerable distance from their own country.'"

NOTE IV.

AS TO BRULÉ BEING THE FIRST WHITE PERSON TO "SHOOT" LACHINE RAPIDS.

"The first white man to descend the rapids of St. Louis [Lachine rapids] was a youth [Brulé, as we assume] who had volunteered, the previous summer, to go with the Hurons to their country and winter among them,—a proposal to which Champlain gladly assented. The second was a young man named Louis, who had gone up with Indians to an island in the rapid, to shoot herons, and was drowned in the descent. The third was Champlain himself."—*Pioneers of France in the New World*, p. 335*n*. But the facts, as related by Champlain, are, that Savignon and a Montagnais, while all were waiting the arrival of the Hurons and Algonquins, started with Louis for the island and, on their return, the latter and the Indian were drowned. This can hardly be considered a descent of the rapids by the unfortunate Frenchman. *Afterward*, Brulé, in company with the Hurons, on his return from their country, "shot" the rapids; and, subsequently, he and Champlain together were safely piloted down by Indians.

NOTE V.

SIGNIFICATION OF THE WORD "CARANTOUANNAIS."

"I have seen only one derivation of the word 'Carantouannais;' and that one seems far-fetched: 'Great tree — Gavónta-(go)-wane.'"— John Gilmary Shea, in *The Pennsylvania Magazine of History and Biography*, vol. II, p. 103. In Gen. John S. Clark's ideal map to be found in Dr. Charles Hawley's *Early Chapters of Cayuga History* (Auburn: 1879), these Indians are mentioned as "Carantouannais, or Onontiogas."

In the edition of 1619, of his *Voyages*, Champlain, in the account of his expedition of 1615, gives no name to these Indians. He speaks of them only as "a certain nation;" so, also, in his Narrative of 1618, in the same edition.

To the edition of Champlain's *Voyages* of 1632 is added a large map of New France, usually spoken of as "Champlain's Map of 1632." On this map are numbers inserted at various localities of note. These refer to an Index in the book having explanations of greater or less extent of the points at which they are placed. The nation just mentioned as living to the south of the Onondagas is named on the map "Carantouannais," and in the Index "Carantouanis." Shea, Slafter, and others, drop one *n*, thus: "Carantouanais." Parkman gives "Carantoüans" in his *Jesuits in North America*, p. XLVI*n* — and "Carantouans" in his *Pioneers of France in the New World*, p. 377. Occasionally, we find some authors writing, "Carantowans."

NOTE VI.

THE CHOUONTOUAROÜON IDENTICAL WITH THE SENECAS.

That the Chouontouaroüon and Senecas were one and the same, see O. H. Marshall, in *The Magazine of American History*, vol. I, pp. 1–5; where, however, he spells the name first mentioned incorrectly. One of the most important facts to prove the correctness of his conclusions — the delineation upon Champlain's Map of 1632, of the circuitous route taken usually by the Hurons in going to their allies upon the Susquehanna river — is overlooked by Mr. Marshall. "This nation [the Carantouannais]," says Champlain, "is very warlike according to the representation of the Attigouautans [Hurons]. They are only three villages in the midst of more than twenty others against which they carry on war, not being able to get assistance from their friends, especially as they [their friends — the Hurons], must pass through the country of the Chouontouaroüon [Senecas], or go a great way round." Champlain uses "Attigouautans" (and sometimes "Attignouaatitans," or "Atinouaentans") for the "Hurons," although, strictly speaking, the name belonged to one only of the five tribes, or clans, of that nation.

NOTE VII.

MARCH OF CHAMPLAIN AND HIS HURONS TO THE ONONDAGA VILLAGE. —CONFLICTING VIEWS AS TO THE SITE OF THE ENEMY'S STRONGHOLD.

"There has always gathered around Champlain's expedition into the land of the Five Nations, a romance inseparable from bold and gallant adventure. It was not perhaps prudent, it was not war, but it was brilliant, and it had all the dash of a zealous explorer, eager to see something new.

"While Virginia was just struggling into life, and the States of Holland were organizing into a government, the few frail structures thrown up at New Amsterdam and Fort Orange, [it was previous to any *permanent* structures at New Amsterdam and before the beginning of Fort Orange], while New England was still a desert, its woods not yet tuned to echo the psalmody of the Puritan, Samuel de Champlain, who had fought too long against the Leaguers in France to relish listless idleness, had explored the New England coast and mapped all its harbors, had founded Quebec, ascended the Ottawa, and reached Lake Huron, had discovered the lake that bears his name, and taken a hand in Indian wars.

"There was just the stir and freshness in it all that charmed him. In 1615, he was at a Huron town near Lake Simcoe, and his Huron and Algonquin allies were planning a great expedition against an enemy who lay beyond Ontario (*the beautiful lake*), in the lake-dotted fertile territory to the south. The town of a tribe, whom he styles in his narrative the Entouohonorons [Entouhonorons], was to be the point of attack. A kindred nation, the Carantouanais . . . stout warriors, living in three towns near the Susquehanna, were to coöperate with the Hurons. Would Champlain take a hand in the matter? Of course he would. . . . .

"Champlain, with the rest of Frenchmen, joined the great Huron war party, and after the usual feasts and dances, the Frenchmen and their dusky allies left the town of Cahiague, their starting-point, north of Lake Simcoe [for the Onondaga stronghold]. . . . .

"The Huron town Cahiague, from which the Huron war party [with Champlain and his French companions] set out, Sept. 1,

1615, was some years later called by the Jesuits St. Jean Baptiste, and though it may have been removed from the original site a few miles, cannot be far from the position given it on Du Creux's map, between Lake Simcoe and Lake Couchiching. They embarked on the latter lake, entered Simcoe, and having . . . sent Brulé with twelve Hurons to the Susquehanna region to notify their allies, they made the portage to Sturgeon Lake, and thence through Pigeon, Buckhorn, Clear, and Rice Lakes, the Ontonabee and Trent Rivers, plying their paddles where there was a good stretch of water, or making a toilsome portage overland at the frequent rapids. They, finally, after 64 leagues' travel, reached Quinte Bay, and sailing up that sheet of water, reached the waters of Lake Ontario."— John Gilmary Shea, in *The Pennsylvania Magazine of History and Biography*, vol. II, pp. 103, 105.

That author also says (same vol., p. 103): "Of this expedition Champlain is our historian, for he was always ready with his pen, and as a trained navigator mapped a coast or country with no little skill and accuracy. His accounts appeared first in a volume of his voyages, published in Paris in 1619, with a picture of the Indian fort [the Onondaga stronghold]; and in an abridged form in a general collection of his voyages, published in the French capital in 1632, and accompanied by a map of New France, on which the course of the expedition over New York soil and the position of the fort which the Hurons and their French allies attacked are laid down.

"The Recollet Sagard wrote, subsequently to the expedition, two works, his 'Great Voyage to the Huron Country,' and his 'History of Canada;' but neither of these volumes throws any further light upon the route pursued, or the citadel which the allies proposed to take. The later work of the Recollet LeClerq, based on manuscripts of Champlain's time, introduces a few new facts, but is too vague to be of any service in the main question [as to the location of the fort]. The documents bearing upon the point are, therefore, Champlain's narrative (1619) [that is, published in that year], the picture of the fort, and the map in the edition of 1632."

There are three points — each one of which has been suggested as the most likely location of the Onondaga village: (1) The right (or east) bank of Onondaga creek, not a great distance south of the present city of Syracuse; (2) the east side of Onondaga lake; (3) Nichols Pond, in the town of Fenner, Madison county.* Other points that have been advocated are now considered as out of the range of a reasonable probability.

* Nichols Pond—in the northeast corner of the town of Fenner, in Madison county, N. Y., three miles east of the village of Perryville, and ten miles by an air line, south of the east end of Oneida lake.

Consult further as to the Onondaga stronghold, John Gilmary Shea, in *The Pennsylvania Magazine of History and Biography*, vol. II, pp. 103-108; O. H. Marshall, in *The Magazine of American History*, vol. I, pp. 6-13, and vol. II, p. 470-483; George Geddes, in same, vol. I, pp. 521-537; E. F. Slafter, in *Prince Society Publications of Champlain's "Voyages,"* vol. I, p. 130n, and in his "Champlain," in *Narrative and Critical History of America*, vol. IV, p. 125; Parkman, in *Pioneers of France in the New World*, p. 373; Justin Winsor, in *Cartier to Frontenac*, pp. 117, 118; and the writers cited by these authors. However, a consideration of this question has but little importance in our narrative except as a help in approximating the location of Carantouan—"three short days' journey south." The most prominent writers to take sides in regard to the locality of the fort, or village, are Gen. John S. Clark and O. H. Marshall.

In his "Champlain," Mr. Slafter (Winsor's *Narrative and Critical History of America*, vol. IV, p. 125) gives, in a sketch-map, both the route advocated by Marshall and the one suggested by Clark, from the point where Champlain first struck the shore of Lake Ontario to the Onondaga village. These routes come together near the outlet of Oneida Lake, Clark's going thence southeast to Nichols Pond and Marshall's southwest to Onondaga lake. (See, also, Winsor's *Cartier to Frontenac*, p. 118.) If, now, Marshall's route be continued about ten miles from the site he advocates to a point on the east bank of the Onondaga creek, not far above the present city of Syracuse, then the place suggested by Geddes will be reached (see his map in *The Magazine of American History*, vol. I, p. 521); but, in going from the fishery to the fort, it is probable Onondaga lake was left some distance to the right (or west).

As there is a general acquiescing on all hands as to the location of the "fishery" being at the outlet of the Oneida lake (and there can be little or no doubt but such was the fact), it is not necessary to go north of this point in what we have now to consider. The mistake made by Marshall, it is suggested, was in stopping short at Onondaga lake; and this was caused without doubt by his not catching the correct idea of Champlain's words. The passage which induced him to "stop short" is sometimes translated thus:

"The ninth of the month of October [1615], our savages, while upon a scout, came upon eleven savages whom they took prisoners — that is to say, four women, three boys, one girl and three men — who were going *to fish at a distance of about four leagues from the enemy's fort* [the italicising is mine]."—

The Magazine of American History, vol. I, p. 566. (See, also, O'Callaghan's *Documentary History of the State of New York*, vol. III, p. 87. That this was the way Marshall understood it, is evident from his words:

"The expedition must have met the party of Iroquois, which included women and children, not far from *the fishery and the village, which were only about four leagues or ten miles apart* [the italicising is mine]."—*The Magazine of American History*, vol. I, p. 12. And he also says (vol. II., p. 478): "On the 9th of October, the Indians met and captured eleven of the enemy, who were going to the fishery, distant 4 leagues from the enemy's fort." And again (same vol., p. 479): "Champlain states that the fort was 4 leagues (10 miles), from the 'fishery,'" And this he substantially repeats.

It is believed, however, that the following is a better translation, and that it conveys the real meaning of Champlain:

"On the 9th of the month of October our savages going out to reconnoitre met eleven savages, whom they took prisoners. They consisted of four women, three boys, one girl, and three men, who were going fishing *and were distant some four leagues from the fort of the enemy* [the italicising is mine]." *

"Here the Canadians [meaning the savages with Champlain] captured eleven Iroquois, who had come about four leagues from their fort to fish in the Oneida lake."—Brodhead's *New York*, (Revised ed.), vol. I., p. 69. But this is error in this that it makes their place of capture also their place of fishing.

In *The Magazine of American History*, vol. I, p. 1, Mr. Marshall gives a "fac-simile of part of the Champlain map of 1632." The size of the Onondaga village as there delineated is out of all proportion with the vicinity in which it was located. It would include the whole of Onondaga lake and creek. This doubtless has misled that writer, as the stronghold (because of the error in its size as marked on the map) is made to reach from the east side of the creek to the east side of the lake.

There is one fact not mentioned by Geddes which adds to his theory: Champlain speaks of the Carantouannais as living three good days' journey, *further up (plus haut)* than the Onondagas, which expression he would hardly have made use of had the stronghold of the enemy been located on a pond or lake; and then, too, going *further up* the Onondaga creek would have been going in the right direction. All things considered, we think Mr. Geddes has much the best of the argument.†

* See Otis's translation of *Champlain's* "*Voyages*," vol. III, p. 128.
† "Absolute identification [of the site of the stronghold of the enemy] is

NOTE VIII.

EARLY MENTION OF THE FALLS OF NIAGARA.

The cataract of Niagara was first heard of in 1535, by Cartier. Then again by Champlain, as we have seen, in 1603.

"Champlain was not ignorant in 1603 of the existence of the falls of Niagara, since La Franchise, who, according to Sulte's "Jean Nicolet," in *Mélanges D'Histoire et de Littérature*, pp. 424, 425, dedicated to him a sonnet, expresses himself thus:

"' Muses si vous chantez vraiment je vous conseille
Que vous louciez Champlain pour être courageux,
Sans crainte des hasards, il a vu tant de lieux
Que ses relations nous contentent l'oreille.

"' Il a vu le Pérou[1] Mexique, et la merveille
Du Vulcain infernal qui vomit tant de feux;
Et les sauts Mocosans[2] qui offensent les yeux
De ceux qui osent voir leur chute nonpareille.'

"Lescarbo wrote in 1310 a piece of verse in which he speaks of the grand falls which the savages say they meet with in ascending the St. Lawrence to the neighborhood of Virginia.

"'[1]Pas que nous sachions.'
"'[2]*Mocosa*, ancien nom de la Virginie, ce qui se rapporterait au Niagara. Pas plus que le Pérou Champlain ne l'avait vu, mais, évidemment, il en avait entendu parler.'"

In the Index to Champlain's Map of 1632, it is said:

"⁹⁰ Sault d'eau au bout du Sault [Lac] Sainct Louis fort haut où plusieurs sortes de poissons descendans s'estourdissent."

[*Translation:* ⁹⁰ A waterfall of considerable height, at the extremity of Lake St. Louis [Ontario], where several kinds of fish are stunned in their descent.]

This note (90) is given to describe the falls of Niagara, which are laid down with considerable correctness on the map.

"Champlain does not appear to have obtained from the Indians any adequate idea of the grandeur and magnificence of this fall. The expression, *qui est quelque peu élevé, où il y a peu d'eau laquelle descend*, would imply that it was of moderate if not of

not possible."—Kingsford: *History of Canada*, vol. I, p. 52. Notwithstanding this declaration (and we heartily subscribe to its truthfulness), Gen. Clark, in advocating Nichols Pond as the true site, says: "I identify the site as certainly as any gentleman present [at a gathering of pioneers in Syracuse] can identify his wife at the breakfast table after ten years of married life" (see *The Magazine of American History*, vol. II, p. 471). This Mr. Marshall answers effectively.

an inferior character."— Rev. E. F. Slafter, in *Prince Society Publications of Champlain's "Voyages,"* vol. I, p. 271*n*. (Mr. Slafter here speaks of what Champlain records of his interview with the savages in 1603, referred to in our Narrative.) See, also, in this connection, Parkman's *Pioneers of France in the New World*, p. 220*n*.

Such a description of the cataract as that given in the Index to Champlain's map makes it highly probable that no white man had seen the falls before the year 1632, notwithstanding the Neutral nation was visited before 1626 by Brulé, and in the year last mentioned by Daillon. (See, in this connection, Note XIX, of this Appendix.) And the former must have gone not many miles from the great cataract, in 1615.

"It will be observed, that we get [from Champlain's map of 1632] in the stream which enters Lake Ontario at the west end the first fairly accurate [cartographical] location of the Niagara cataracts. Champlain never comprehended the magnitude of these falls any more than Cartier did when he seems to have heard of them, a hundred years before. Sanson, when he published his map of 1656, represented the conception of Champlain; but we get no particular [cartographical] description of the cataract till we find one, drawn from hearsay, however, . . . in Galinée's journal, when this priest accompanied La Salle along Lake Ontario in 1669."—Winsor: *Cartier to Frontenac*, p. 144.

NOTE IX.

BRULÉ'S DISCOVERY OF LAKES HURON AND ONTARIO.

"In the year 1615, there dwelt on the south-eastern shore of Lake Huron, between Lake Simcoe and the Georgian Bay, a nation of Indians who were called in their own language, 'Wendats' or 'Wyandots,' and by the French 'Hurons.' There is no record of their having been visited by the white man prior to the above date."— O. H. Marshall, in *The Magazine of American History*, vol. I, p. 1. But this statement that no white man had, previous to 1615, visited the "Wendats" (Hurons), was made by that writer from having overlooked the journey of Champlain's "lad," and that of another young Frenchman subsequently.

Even Parkman forgets the journey of Champlain's "servant," in heading Chapter XIII, of his *Pioneers of France in the New World* (p. 357), with,— "1615. Discovery of Lake Huron,"— as if it were discovered in that year; when, in the same volume, p. 335*n*, he speaks of "a youth who had volunteered, the previous summer [i. e., in the summer of 1610], *to go with the Hurons to their country and winter among them,— a proposal to which Champlain* gladly assented." (The italicising is mine.) And, as we have shown, another young Frenchman went on a journey to Lake Huron and to the country of the Wendats (Hurons), the year following the one in which Brulé made his visit there. As Father Le Caron and his French escort preceded Champlain and his two white companions some days in reaching, in 1615, that lake, the first mentioned persons would be entitled to the honor of having been its discoverers, had they not been preceded themselves by Brulé and another, as just related.

The first European to gain any knowledge of Lake Ontario was James Cartier, in 1635. He was then on the St. Lawrence and his information was given him by savages. He was told that, after ascending many leagues among rapids and waterfalls, he would reach a lake one hundred and fifty leagues long and forty or fifty broad [Lake Ontario], at the western extremity of which the waters were wholesome and the winters mild; that a river [Niagara] emptied into it from the south, which had its source in the country of the Iroquois; that beyond this lake he would find a cataract and portage [Niagara Falls and the land-route around the cataract]; then another lake [Erie] about equal to the former, which they had never explored, and still further on a sea [probably Lake Huron].*

Again, in 1603, the lake was heard of, but this time by Champlain, who says: "Then they [the Indians who gave him the account] come to a lake [Ontario] some eighty leagues long, with a great many islands; the water at its extremity being fresh and the winter mild. At the end of this lake they pass a fall [Niagara], somewhat high and with but little water flowing over. Here they carry their canoes overland about a quarter of a league, in order to pass the fall, afterwards entering another lake [Erie] some sixty leagues long, and containing very good water. Having reached the end, they come to a strait [Detroit and St. Clair rivers] two leagues broad and extending a considerable distance into the interior. They said they had never gone any farther nor seen the end of a lake [Huron] some fifteen or sixteen leagues distant from where they had been."†

In another account given Champlain by "two or three Algonquins," he was informed that, after leaving the river they were then on, a lake would be reached (Lake Ontario), some hundred and fifty (French) leagues in length. Not far above the foot of

*Lescarbot's *Histoire de la Nouvelle France* (1609), p. 381.
† *Prince Society Publications of Champlain's "Voyages,"* vol. I, p. 271.

this lake there could be seen a river (bay of Quinté) extending towards the north to the Algonquins; that there was another river (the Oswego), coming from the Iroquois country — where the Algonquins and Iroquois make war upon each other. A little farther along on the south shore of the lake would be seen another river (the Genesee), also extending towards the Iroquois. At the end of the lake a fall (Niagara) would be reached where the Indians were obliged to carry their canoes. Beyond this, another very large lake would soon be entered (Lake Erie), as long, perhaps, as the first. They said they had seldom seen the lake last mentioned but they had heard that beyond was another great water; this, however, they had not seen.*

Lake Ontario was first cartographically sketched in the Molineaux map of 1600, where it is spoken of as "The Lacke of Tadenac, the bounds whereof are unknown,"— merged, however, into "a great inland sea, the prototype of the Great Lakes."†

In a map drawn by Champlain in 1612, the lake is located in nearly its exact position,— a description of it having been obtained from Indian accounts previously given him.‡ Upon this map, Lake St. Peter, "Mont Royale" (Montreal), the St. Lawrence, and the Lachine rapids, together with the Richelieu river, Lake Champlain, Lake Ontario, Niagara falls, and Oneida lake, are, most of them, fairly well indicated. The Ottawa river is recognizable; so, also (but with a considerable draft upon the imagination), are Lakes Nipissing and Simcoe and the French river. Lake Huron as "grand lac" is made intelligible — the location of a Huron village on its southeastern shore being plainly represented. A short water-course leads out of the foot of Lake Huron to the head of Lake Ontario — Champlain having too indistinct a knowledge of Lake Erie to give it a place on this map, or even on the ones of 1632.

Some writers assert that Champlain was the first white man to reach Lake Ontario:

"The discovery of Lake Ontario, in 1615, was an ample compensation for previous disappointments in his [Champlain's] indefatigable explorations. . . . Champlain was the first European who visited the 'fresh-water sea,' as he called Ontario."— Garneau's *History of Canada* (Bell's translation), vol. I, p. 92. But Champlain called Lake Huron the *Mer Douce*, not Lake Ontario.

* Id., p. 274.
† Winsor's *Narrative and Critical History of America*, vol. IV, p. 377.
‡ Winsor's *Cartier to Frontenac*, pp. 103, 104.

SECTION OF CHAMPLAIN'S LARGE MAP OF 1612.

APPENDIX.

The same view as to Champlain having been the first to discover Lake Ontario is taken by William Kingsford, in his *History of Canada*, vol. I, pp. 50, 51. But Champlain's own narrative is a sufficient evidence that Brulé was before him in reaching "the beautiful lake," and this, too, whether his route was by way of its foot or its head.

Historians have been chary of committing themselves as to the route pursued by Brulé after leaving Champlain. "Crossing Lake Ontario," says Parkman (*Pioneers of France in the New World*, p. 377, the "party [Brulé and the twelve Hurons] pushed on with all speed," etc.; but as to *where* the party crossed the lake, he does not venture an opinion. However, as suggested by us, it is probable the Frenchman and his savages did not cross Ontario at all, but coasted around its head to the mouth of the Niagara. Winsor (*Cartier to Frontenac*, p. 117) gives it as a possibility that Brulé pursued the course indicated by a dotted line in Champlain's map of 1632, which would necessitate his going at least *towards the head of the lake and beyond it*. But what is a possibility with Mr. Winsor is a reality with the Rev. E. F. Slafter (in *Prince Society Publications of Champlain's "Voyages,"* vol. III, p. 208*n*). Now, for the party to have gone from the point where Champlain and his savages had rendezvoused, in that general direction without seeing Lake Ontario would be incredible — indeed, wellnigh impossible; and if seen, it must have been before it was reached on the other route by Champlain.

NOTE X.

EARLY REPORTS OF LAKE ERIE.

Cartier, as we have shown, was the first of civilized men to receive an inkling of the existence of Lake Erie. This was in 1535. Champlain had, when, in 1629, he made his large map of New France, no knowledge of it, except by vague Indian reports of 1603, which gave him apparently a most confused idea of it. The accounts he then obtained from the savages are given in Note IX of this Appendix. It is but reasonable to suppose that had Brulé visited the lake on his journey to, or return from the Carantouannais, Champlain would have given a better drawing of it in his map just mentioned.

NOTE XI.

THE HOME OF THE ERIES.

The Eries were of the Iroquois family. When first heard of they occupied the southern shore of the lake to which their name has been given. Their territory extended nominally as far east as the Genesee river in what is now the State of New York, and as far west, probably, as the Sandusky and Scioto rivers in the present State of Ohio. Their villages, it is conjectured, were not far from the western boundary of the former State, as now defined. How far south this nation had its hunting-grounds, tradition and history give no account. From the known location of other nations, it is presumed, however, their territory included the region watered by the Alleghany. How long this extensive country had been occupied by the Eries is beyond the reach of any historic record. No tradition has been preserved of their migration to this section. However, as kindred nations usually pointed to the St. Lawrence as the spot once their hunting-grounds, it is not improbable that they too were from the great valley of the north.

Doubtless, the Eries were heard of by Captain Smith while exploring the Chesapeake bay in 1608,* and by Brulé in his journey to the Carantouannais, although even at as late a date as 1632 very little was known of them as a distinct nation. And at no time until the first half of the seventeenth century had passed was there anything of moment concerning them made known to Europeans.

NOTE XII.

GRAND DETOUR FROM THE HURON COUNTRY TO THE SUSQUEHANNA.

The lengthy and circuitous route taken by the savages in going from the St. Lawrence to the Virginia country, in order to avoid the hostile Iroquois, is early noted. It is referred to on Captain John Smith's map of Virginia of 1612 (by inference), from data obtained four or five years before, also in his *Génerall Historie of Virginia* of 1624, from the same early information; and in 1610, Lescarbot, in his *La Nouvelle France*, also mentions this great circuit made by the Indians, for the purpose of trade.

Now, at or near the mouth of the Niagara river, there commenced a branch route running northerly to the country of the Hurons. This route was made known to Champlain in 1611 by the savages just mentioned, who said they had been visited by friendly Indians from beyond the south side of the territory oc-

---

*Capt. John Smith, in his map of Virginia (Oxford: 1612), lays down the "Vitchowig" (probably the Eries), at the head of the upper West Branch of the Susquehanna; but it is probable the Indians, in giving him an account of the nation and of the location of their towns, mentioned the West Branch as being followed to its head when one would journey to that nation from the Susquehanna.

cupied by the unfriendly Iroquois. It is believed the Indians occupying the country near Lake Simcoe journeyed south on the Humber; thence, on Lake Ontario to the mouth of the Niagara river; up that stream to the great cataract (where a portage was made to the river above); thence to the foot of Lake Erie; coasting then on the southern side of Lake Erie to where the city of Erie (Pennsylvania) is now located; making a portage again and going down French creek to the Alleghany; thence up that river to near its head waters, where there were two portages — one leading across to the Tioga, the other across to the head of the West Branch of the Susquehanna (both tributaries of the latter). As the Tioga leads into the Chemung, and the latter flows into the Susquehanna near what is now the north boundary line of the State of Pennsylvania, there was, of course, canoe navigation all the way to the Carantouannais. The West Branch having its confluence with the parent stream much farther down, made a channel of communication to the Susquehanna proper and to the country below.

This wide circuit (or " grand detour ") was taken by a party of Hurons after the period of Brulé's journey, both in going to the Indians upon the Susquehanna and in returning home after visiting them, to avoid the Senecas.— Parkman: *The Jesuits in North America*, pp. 341 - 343. "They [the Hurons]," says this author (p. 343), "were forced to make a wide sweep through the Alleghanies, Western Pennsylvania and apparently Ohio, to avoid these vigilant foes [the Senecas]."

On Champlain's map of 1632 is a dotted line reaching from Lake Erie to the Susquehanna; — that is, from what, it seems, is intended as that lake, to the river. Now, some writers have supposed that this line was made to represent Brulé's route to the Carantouannais. "A dotted line will be seen on the same map [Champlain's map, of 1632], evidently intended to mark the course of Brulé's journey. From the meagre knowledge which Champlain possessed of the region, the line can hardly be supposed to be very accurate."— E. F. Slafter, in *Prince Society Publications of Champlain's "Voyages,"* vol. III, p. 208*n*. "Brulé volunteered to reach them [the Carantouannais]. He succeeded in passing the hostile villages of the Iroquois, possibly by the route indicated by the dotted line in Champlain's map of 1632."—Winsor, in *Cartier to Frontenac*, p. 117. (See Note IX of this Appendix.) That the line mentioned commences so far from the head of Lake Ontario,— evidently beyond and to the south of some Indian villages lying east of the Niagara river, and that it branches before reaching Carantouan, pretty conclusively proves that it was intended to indicate, not Brulé's route, but the grand circuit before spoken of, which the party had not time to follow.

NOTE XIII.

CAPTAIN JOHN SMITH'S DISCOVERY OF THE SUSQUEHANNA.—DID HE REACH PENNSYLVANIA?

It is certain the river to which Capt. John Smith first gave the name of "Smith's Falls" is the stream now known as the Susquehanna; for, besides the descriptions given in his account of its discovery, the river where it empties into the Chesapeake bay is so faithfully delineated by him in a map which he made soon after as to leave no doubt of its identity.

As to the distance Captain Smith journeyed up the Susquehanna from its mouth, the principal authority is the Captain himself; first, in his *Description of the Countrey* of Virginia (Oxford: 1612); and, second, in his *Génerall Histoire of Virginia* (London: 1640):

"At the end of the [Chesapeake] bay, where it is six or seven miles in breadth, there fall into it four small rivers,—three of them issuing from divers bogs [marshes or swamps], environed with high mountains. There is one [the Susquehanna] that cometh [from] due north, three or four days' journey from the head of the bay, and falls from rocks and mountains."

"At the end of the [Chesapeake] bay, where it is six or seven miles in breadth, it divides itself into four branches, the best cometh northwest from among the mountains; but, though canoes may go a day's journey or two up it [the Susquehanna], we could not get two miles up it with our boat, for rocks."

That canoes could go, possibly, two days' journey up the river, is a declaration having much force, in view of the fact that it is about forty miles from its mouth before what are now known as "Conewago falls" are reached; but it is probable that Smith did not quite understand the situation as depicted by the savages, who doubtless said two days' journey would take them to a point where a portage would have to be made.*

*"At the end of the [Chesapeake] Bay where it is 6 or 7 miles in breadth, there fall into it 4 small rivers, 3 of them issuing from divers bogges invironed with high mountaines.

"There is one that commeth du north, 3 or 4. daies iourny from the head of the Bay, and fals from rocks and mountaines. Vpon this river inhabit a people called *Sasquesahanock*.

"They [the Sasquesahanocks] are seated 2 daies higher then was passage for the discoverers Barge, which was hardly 2 toons, and had in it but 12 men

APPENDIX.   145

The Susquehanna river takes its name from the nation of Indians which were found inhabiting its valley in 1608 and which, by Captain Smith were called, as we have seen, "Sasquesahanocks." These savages had their home in the vicinity of some falls — their name signifying probably, "the Falls People," or, "They who live at the falls." The distance of their town from the mouth of the Susquehanna, as given by Smith, corresponds, approximately, to that of the Conewago falls from the same point — two days' canoe-journey. "The Sasquesahanocks," says the Captain, "inhabit upon the chief spring of these four branches of the bay's head [that is, upon the Susquehanna], two days' journey higher than our barge could pass for rocks." And, again: "Upon this river [the Susquehanna] inhabit a people called Sasquesahanock. They are seated two days' [journey] higher than was passage for the discoverer's barge." Smith also declares that, in sending from the mouth of the river, two Tockwogh Indians to the Sasquesahanocks, inviting the latter to visit him, he expected the messengers would return in "three or four days;" which would be about the time he might expect them, taking into consideration the distance of their town from where he lay with his barge, — *then*, sixty of those savages appeared, as he had calculated (*Histoire*, vol. I, Chap. VI)."

"Capt. Smith," says Prof. Guss, "passed up the Susquehanna to the falls. He says. 'Though canoes may go a day's journey or two up it, we could not get two miles up it with our boats for rocks.' The first rocks, however, we now know, are Port Deposit, at the head of tide water, and this point is four miles from the bay. It is very probable, also, that Smith was up still higher, either on land or in an Indian canoe. The number of islands in the river, which he has marked on his map, and the cross mark

to perform this discouery."—*A Map of Virginia. VVith a description of the Covntrey*, etc. "Written by Captaine Smith, sometimes Governour of the Countrey." Oxford: 1612, p. 7. Arber's Reprint (1884), p. 53. (The map is reprinted in Winsor's *Narrative and Critical History of America*, vol. IV, p. 167; also, in Sharf's *Maryland*, vol. I, p. 6; in the *Historical Register*, vol. I, p. 161; and in other works.)

This tract, as it is called (i.e., "A map of Virginia," etc., just described), contains one hundred and fifty-eight pages,—the "Description of the Covntrey," by Smith, forty-eight pages, and an "Appendix," by other writers, one hundred and ten pages. In this work is published for the first time an account of the Susquehanna river, and of a nation of savages called "Sasquesahanocks," who had, in 1608, their homes on that stream.

A previous work by **Smith**, the *True Relation*, published in London, in 1608, has not, of course, any mention of his explorations in the Chesapeake of that year; yet it contains information obtained from Powhatan the year previous of considerable interest as bearing upon events subsequently described by the Captain.

denoting the highest point reached by him on the river, being by the scale at least fifteen miles, seem to require that Capt. Smith was actually up as far as the State line. On the Potomac and other rivers it is clear he went beyond the 'rocks.' He may have been the first white man that ever trod the soil of Pennsylvania. At all events, so far as we have any definite account, he was the first white man that met Indians who resided within the limits of Pennsylvania."—(*Historical Register*, vol. I, pp. 163, 164).

"The Susquehannocks of Smith . . . are placed, in his map, on the east side of the Susquehanna, some twenty miles from its mouth."— Parkman: *The Jesuits in North America*, p. 311*n*. Prof. Guss places them, *according to the map*, twenty-two miles (*Historical Register*, vol. I, p. 165). He says: "The principal town, Sasquesahanough, is laid down on the map [Smith's], by the scale, about twenty-two miles from the bay." Does not this fact "seem to require" as strongly that the Sasquesahanock town was only that distance from the mouth of the river as those other facts mentioned by him "seem to require that Capt. Smith was up as far as the State line?" We think so; for he immediately adds: "But the book [Capt. Smith's] speaks of them being located 'two days' journey higher than our barge could pass for the rocks,' which would place them [the Sasquesahanoacks] much higher up the river. Certainly, a two days' journey was more than twenty-two miles, and as they awaited the return of the interpreters [the two Tockwogh Indians] 'three or four days,' they probably may have gone forty or fifty miles."

But Prof. Guss strives to break the force of his own arguments by subsequently declaring that "no dependence can be placed upon the scale of leagues [found in Smith's map] for points beyond the limits of Smith's explorations." Now, as "the limits of Smith's explorations" are declared by himself to be within two miles from the mouth of the river, "what dependence can be placed upon the scale of leagues," which places them "at least fifteen miles" from the bay—"as far up as the State line?"

But Prof. Guss thinks it very probable that Smith was up still further than a point "four miles" from its mouth, "either on land or in an Indian canoe." But this was his first visit to the Susquehanna, and he had not seen Indians for a considerable length of time; it is clear, therefore, he had no Indian canoe. That he could not have left his barge and traveled farther up the river bank is evident from several circumstances: (1) He had lost his anchor; (2) half his men were sick; (3) he gives no description of the country along the shore; (4) he did not know then but Indians might be near and make it dangerous to leave his boat; and (5) it seems, from his narrative, he returned to the bay before another tide.

NOTE XIV.

CONCERNING BRULÉ'S EXPLORATION OF THE SUSQUEHANNA RIVER AND THE CHESAPEAKE BAY.

Rev. Edward D. Neill, A. B., in Winsor's *Narrative and Critical History of America*, vol. IV, p. 165, says: "[Brulé] told Champlain that he had found a river which he descended until it flowed into a sea,—the river by some supposed to be the Susquehanna, and the sea Chesapeake bay,"—that writer citing Parkman's *Pioneers*, pp. 377, 378. It is proper, however, to remark that the narrative of Brulé as related by Champlain speaks rather of *the* sea instead of *a* sea, and also that Parkman does not mention the Chesapeake. But the Rev. E. F. Slafter thinks "the sea" mentioned by Brulé to Champlain was the Chesapeake: "He [Brulé] appears to have gone as far south at least as the upper waters of Chesapeake bay."—(*Prince Society Publications of Champlain's "Voyages,"* vol. III, p. 211n.)

Neill seems not to be entirely satisfied that Brulé's declaration with regard to finding "a river which he descended until it flowed into a sea" was a fact,—that "he may have depended upon his imagination." But a careful analysis of the information imparted to Champlain by his interpreter concerning his journey leaves no room for the belief that it was the work of the explorer's imagination, unless, possibly, in this, that he viewed the Chesapeake as simply a continuation of the Susquehanna—a widening of that river, an idea Champlain got from Brulé's recital, as appears not only by what he says of the story of the latter, but by his (Champlain's) map of 1632. It is altogether certain that the narrowness of the Chesapeake at its head must have shown Brulé at once that it was not the ocean, although there was a tide there. Besides, in journeying down the bay, he would be constantly made aware that it was not the Atlantic. Then, too, he could have had no difficulty whatever in learning of the savages, just when and where the ocean would be seen.

NOTE XV.

SOUTHERN AND WESTERN IROQUOIS.

It has been suggested in this narrative that all the savage nations who lived south of the Five Nations and who had a language akin to the Iroquois might properly be classed, generically, as Southern Iroquois. In 1615, they occupied a large extent of territory, extending as far east as the Delaware river and as far south as the Carolinas. And it may here be suggested that, with equal propriety, the Hurons, the Neutrals, the Eries, and the Petuns, might be set down as Western Iroquois. We have, then, three divisions of the Iroquois-speaking people: (1) the Iroquois proper (or Five Nations); (2) the Western Iroquois; and, (3) the Southern Iroquois.

The reason for the conflicting statements of writers as to the Southern Iroquois can, in the light of recent investigations, be readily accounted for. It has been taken for granted that, because of these nations being closely related linguistically, many of them were confederated who were not in any manner leagued together; and, frequently, some of these nations known by different names have been considered as one and the same, when, in fact, they were wholly distinct.

Prof. Guss (in the *Historical Register*, vol. I, p. 40), in considering the Iroquois generally, says: "When the writer a few years since first promulgated before the Anthropological Society of Washington the idea that Iroquois-speaking tribes extended, originally, continuously from the Five Nations to the Tuscaroras, it was new to others, and a deduction of his own. Others have since adopted this view." He continues (pp. 43-45):

"The Iroquois family may be said to have consisted of the following: the Hurons, comprising four divisions; the Tionontates, or Dinondadies [Tobacco Nation], of Upper Canada; the Attiwandaronks, or Neuter Nation, of the Niagara river region; the Eries, or Cats, of the region south of the east part of Lake Erie. The most memorable member of this family was the Five Nations, consisting of Canningoes, or Mohawks, the Oneidas, the Onondagas, the Cayugas, and the Senecas, or Sonnontowans, who lived in a line as here named, in the central part of western New York, stretching from the Mohawk to the Genesee river. Before this they are said to have extended down the St. Lawrence river to Montreal. They made more history than all the other tribes put together. To relate the Indian history of the Susquehanna, or in fact of all Pennsylvania, is but to repeat some chapters in the annals of the Five Nations. They held the geographical key to the whole country and by their course handed it over to the rule of the Anglo-Saxon races.

"Immediately south of the Five Nations were the Carantowans [Carantouannais, of our narrative], on the borders of Pennsylvania, and allied with the Hurons in wars against the Five

Nations. At Wyoming were the Scahentoarrunon, or people of the Great Flats; on the West Branch were the Otzinachson, or people of the Demons' Dens; on the Juniata were the Onojutta-Haga, or Standing Stone people; below the mountains, on the river and branches, were the Susquehannocks, extending to the Potomac river. In Virginia, above the falls of the Rappahannock, according to Capt. John Smith, were the Mannahoacks, in an alliance with the Monacans, whom Jefferson says were the Tuscaroras, then occupying the heads of the James river, and extending to the Neuse, Tar, and Roanoke rivers. The Chowanokes, or Chowans, the Meherrins, and the Nottaways, on the rivers still bearing the same names, were also members of this Iroquois family. Though once numerous, they soon melted away through contagious diseases, intoxication, and wars, until they were obliterated, or their remnants were incorporated into surviving tribes. The Tuscaroras were further inland. In a war with the whites in 1711-14, some of them were driven out, and were protected on the Juniata river, for ten years, by the Five Nations, and then taken to New York and admitted as a sixth member of the confederacy, which after this was generally called the Six Nations. The remnants left in the south kept going north to join the main body, for fifty-five years afterwards.

"In 1640 the Dutch at Albany and New York began to furnish the Five Nations large quantities of fire-arms, but refused them to the other tribes. This was a wise stroke of policy as to the contiguous Indians, and the French settled beyond in Canada, and also as to securing the much-coveted fur trade. When, in 1665, the English superseded the Dutch, they continued the same policy. These arms gave them a tremendous advantage over the other tribes, and enabled them to destroy their enemies, and commence a high career of conquest and military glory. They seemed especially severe upon the tribes of their own linguistic stock, whose conquered remnants were incorporated into their own towns, and served to augment their strength. They devastated the Hurons in 1649, the Neuter Nation in 1651, and the Eries in 1655. Remnants of Tionontates, called also Petuns, or Tobacco Nation, and some refugees from the above tribes, traveled westward as far as Wisconsin; and, in later years, returned to the regions south of the westward part of Lake Erie, where they were known as the Wyandots. Some of the Huron refugees sought protection under the French at Montreal, where their descendants still reside.

"The various tribes of Pennsylvania, whom the French often generically termed Andastes, Gandastogues, etc., were also extirpated, but the exact dates are unknown, as they were beyond the reach of the missionary and explorer. Some of them probably were destroyed even prior to the Hurons. When, in 1663, the tribes on the upper branches having been disposed of, the Five Nations came to the Susquehannocks, or Minquas, below the mountains; they found them able to withstand their assaults, for they had also been armed by the Swedes first, and afterwards by the Marylanders. However, in 1676, deserted by their white friends, they, too, succumbed to the New York conquerors; and part of their remnants being left upon the old ground as a tributary outpost, were long known as the Conestogas. These conquests were also extended far down into Virginia, and their conquest rights to these lands were paid for by Maryland and Virginia at the treaty in Lancaster, in 1744.

"The central part of Pennsylvania remained long an uninhabited interior, used as a hunting ground by the Five Nations, and as a shelter for their friends. After their conquests southward, their arms were turned westward to the Illinois, and other western tribes; and their rights to those immense regions, as far as the Mississippi river, by virtue of these conquests, were sold to the king of Great Britain, and placed under the Province of New York, and constituted the basis of the English claims, which culminated in the French and Indian war, and through it to the final relinquishment of all the French possessions east of the Mississippi river."

NOTE XVI.

AS TO BRULÉ'S ARRIVAL AT THREE RIVERS IN 1618 AND HIS INTERVIEW THERE WITH CHAMPLAIN.

In the *Prince Society Publications of Champlain's "Voyages,"* vol. I, p. 143, Mr. Slafter says that Champlain did not hear from Brulé for three years after leaving the Huron country for Carantouan: "Champlain made voyages to New France both in 1617 and in 1618. In the latter year, among the Indians who came to Quebec for the purpose of trade, appeared Étienne Brulé, the interpreter, who it will be remembered had been despatched in 1615, when Champlain was among the Hurons, to the Entouhonorons at Carantouan, to induce them to join in the attack of the Iroquois in central New York. During the three years that had intervened, nothing had been heard from him." The learned author subsequently corrects "Entouhonorons" to "Carantouanais;" but, as to the other error, that Champlain did not hear from Brulé, "during the three years that had intervened,"—this he fails to set right. It will be noticed, also, that he says the Indians, among whom was Brulé, "came to Quebec;" but it was to Three Rivers.

The narrative of Brulé is given by Champlain with this introduction:

"Now there was with them [the savages at Three Rivers, who had come down the Ottawa to traffic with the French] a man named Étienne Brulé, one of our interpreters, who had been living with them for eight years, as well to pass his time as to see the country and learn their language and mode of life. He is the one whom we had despatched with orders to go in the direction of the Éntouhonorons [Onondagas] to Carantoüan in order to bring with him the five hundred warriors they [the Carantouannais] had promised to send to our assistance in the war in which we were engaged against their enemies. . . . I called this man . . . and asked him why he did not bring the five hundred men to our assistance in time and what was the cause of the delay; also, why he had not made me a report. Thereupon, he gave me a narrative of his explorations, the particulars of which it will not be out of place to give. He is more to be pitied than blamed for not reporting to me before, because of the misfortunes which he experienced on his journeyings."*

The month during which, in the early days of France, the trade of the Ottawa was prosecuted on the St. Lawrence was July, and was largely carried on in 1618, and for a number of years after, where the town of Three Rivers now stands, but which was not then founded. The village proper began in 1633, and Champlain commenced the erection of a fort there in 1634.

NOTE XVII.

AS TO THE RELIABILITY OF BRULÉ'S NARRATIVE.

"Brulé," says Slafter (vol. I, p.143—*Prince Society Publications of Champlain's "Voyages"*), "related the story of his extraordinary adventures, which Champlain has preserved and which may be found in the report of the voyage of 1618."
. . . "The character of Étienne Brulé, either for honor or veracity," continues Mr. Slafter (p. 143*n*), "is not improved by his subsequent conduct." [the writer here referring to Brulé having subsequently 'sold himself to the English,' mention of which is made in Chapter VIII of our narrative]. That writer adds: "Whether this conduct, base certainly as it was, ought

---

*This is rather a free translation of Champlain's words; but it is believed to convey his real meaning.

to affect the credibility of his story, the reader must judge. Champlain undoubtedly believed it when he first related it to him. He probably had no means then or afterwards of testing its truth. In the edition of 1632, Brulé's story is omitted. It does not necessarily follow that it was omitted because Champlain came to discredit the story, since many passages contained in his preceding publications are omitted in the edition of 1632, but they are not generally passages of so much geographical importance as this, if it be true. The map of 1632 indicates the country of the Carantouanais; but this information might have been obtained by Champlain from the Hurons, or the more western tribes which he visited during the winter of 1615-16.- *Vide* ed. 1632, p. 220."

It is quite inconceivable that by Brulé selling "himself to the English" in 1629 it could affect his narrative as to its reliability, in 1618. Besides, the fact that a part of Brulé's story is confirmed in advance by Brulé's Carantouannais guides is, in the foregoing, overlooked by Mr. Slafter. This author also says: "They [Champlain's interpreters] were generally . . . . adventurers, whose honesty and fidelity had no better foundation than their selfish interests. Of this sort was Étienne Brulé, as well as Nicholas Marsolet and Pierre Raye, all of whom turned traitors, selling themselves to the English when Quebec was taken in 1629" (see vol. III, of the *Prince Society Publications of Champlain's "Voyages,"* p. 216*n*). This is certainly a severe arraignment of these men. As to the "selfish interest" of Brulé, surely few men living could have had less, judging by his zeal, self-denial, courage, and faithfulness, in carrying out the wishes of Champlain. And it is evident that his patron was abundantly satisfied of his "honesty and fidelity" in all that appertained to his journeys undertaken and carried forward with such indomitable perseverance.

That Champlain had anything to do with the omission of Brulé's narrative in his edition of 1632 is doubtful. It was probably done by an "alien hand,"—one who was at least not anxious (and the Jesuits certainly, at that time, were of that class) to give to the world again the particulars of his (Brulé's) journey. But if it was the work of Champlain, it must have been prompted by ill feeling towards his interpreter, caused by the latter having gone over to the English at the period of their taking possession of Canada. In conclusion, we may say that the fact of the narrative having been repeated by Brulé to the historian Sagard after the lapse of at least six years, substantially as given to Champlain, ought to remove all doubts (if such exist in the mind of any one), as to its truthfulness. (See Note XXII [c] of this Appendix.)

"It was during Champlain's sojourn in the valley [of the St. Lawrence] in 1618 that his old interpreter, Étienne Brulé, returned to the settlement [that is, to Three Rivers]. The governor had last seen him when he was dispatched from the Huron company to bring the Andastes [and who were really the Carantouannais] to the attack on the Iroquois fort [of the Onondagas], three years before. Brulé had now the opportunity to disclose the cause of his failure [to bring the five hundred allies, by us spoken of as Carantouannais, to the help of Champlain and his savages], and to explain his later wanderings. It appeared that when Brulé finally brought the Andastes [the 500 Carantouannais] to the neighborhood of the Iroquois stronghold it was only to learn that the Hurons had departed, and there was no alternative left but a like retreat on their part. Brulé remained the following winter with his savage friends, but later, it would appear, he passed down the Susquehanna, to Chesapeake bay, and by this adventure he had established the direction of its course. . . . In making his return journey [from Carantouan], the wanderer fell among the Iroquois. He was wont to point to his wounds to show that he had undergone tortures at their hands. His own story betrays an abundance of tact in ingratiating himself with savages wherever he went. His spirit and facile habit served to convert the Iroquois enmity into a liking for him, and they made it easy for him to reach the Huron country, whence he could join the summer flotilla, descending the Ottawa."—Winsor, in *Cartier to Frontenac*, pp. 121, 122.

Mr. Winsor certainly gives full credit to Brulé's story. But that Brulé passed the winter of 1615-16 not with his savage friends—the Carantouannais, but in exploring the Susquehanna and Chesapeake, is evident.

The following amusing account of Brulé's capture by the Iroquois while returning from Carantouan in 1616, and of his escape from torture, as already related (see, ante, Chap. VII.), is from the pen of the learned historian, Mr. Benjamin Sulte, of Ottawa, Canada (see the Ottawa *Evening Journal*, Oct. 29, 1892):

"Accompanied by five or six Andastes [Carantouannais] the courageous explorer [Brulé] started on his journey to Upper Canada and he must have chosen the same road as before, because those folks captured him after dispersing his escort.

"The first trick Brulé played on the red devils was to affirm that he was an Iroquois himself and that he had escaped slavery with the Andastes [Carantouans]. This gave him a little rest and time to prepare a strategical plan. His skin had certainly turned to the proper color during the last twelve months and his dress and manners were of the Indian stamp; but his language betrayed him a little; his accent proclaimed him a Huron; therefore a bitter enemy. This being found, there was great fun in store for the good people of the village.

"Brulé was asked to be kind enough to trot at a moderate pace between two lines of bastinadoes, and he got a reasonable dose of strokes all over the body. Next, they requested him to jump over a large fire and he performed this exercise with difficulty on account of the breadth of the furnace in question. Thirdly, the 'shake hands' was proceeded with, and Brulé got rid of four or five of his nails during the act of courtesy, for the Iroquois were very liberally inclined in that direction.

"The wind-up of the whole programme was to be the burning at the stake; but Brulé kept cool, with an eye to business. The tormentors had not perceived the coming on of a tremendous summer storm, which suddenly darkened the horizon and Brulé had calculated upon the effect of the weather as well as on his own eloquence. Consequently he assumed the attitude of a prophet, sorcerer or conjurer, as he had seen done amongst the wild Indians, and declared he was not a Huron, but a French spirit from the other side of the world; that he had come to punish the rascally Iroquois and destroy them to the last one. His speech frightened some of them when he revealed his origin, but the threats he uttered, coupled with the crash and fire-serpents from heaven, which followed immediately, caused them to tremble and fly away.

"Brulé was cut loose, of course, but he did not run; on the contrary, he re-entered the village soon after the storm was over, and made a call in proper style to have a general meeting of the population. This being done, he delivered them a long speech, showing the French were next of kin to the angels, or good spirits of Paradise, and that the Dutch [who were then at what is now Albany, New York] were the bad Manitous, and so forth. The Iroquois showed they appreciated his wonderful cleverness by treating him like a supernatural being; and when he left, they did all they could to help him during his journey. They parted with him after four days of travel together."

NOTE XVIII.
CONCERNING BRULÉ'S DISCOVERY OF LAKE SUPERIOR.

It has been shown that Champlain was very anxious in 1616 and in 1618 to solve the problem of the "North Sea," information of which he supposed he had obtained from the savages, while the latter were only giving a confused account of Lake Superior. It has also been explained that Brulé was urged to continue what Champlain had found was impracticable for himself to accomplish — a further exploration in 1615; that an additional journey was to be made northward and northwestward of the Huron country; and that the principal object was the solving of the problem of the "North Sea"— which, in fact, was Lake Superior. It has likewise been seen, that, in 1618, Brulé promised Champlain to proceed at once to comply with his wishes as to a further exploration, and that, in all probability, he soon made a journey up the shores of the North Channel to the nation of the Beaver, returning not later to the St. Lawrence than in the summer of 1620. That the Beavers had knowledge of the nations afterward known as the Menomonees and Winnebagoes, also of the Mascoutins and Sioux, seems altogether probable. That Brulé heard of them on his journey is also likely; and that the latter would naturally gain considerable knowledge of regions lying around the head of Lake Huron, at least enough to increase his desire to visit them, is what might reasonably be expected.

We are now brought to the main question — did Brulé, in a subsequent journey, reach Lake Superior?

Champlain, for the eighth time, now made his appearance in the valley of the St. Lawrence, from France. It was July 7, 1620; and he remained in Canada a little over four years before again embarking for his native country. It is reasonable to suppose that he had not lost interest in distant exploration of savage countries, promoting, as he still was, to the extent of his capabilities, the fur trade. His trusted interpreter, Brulé, must make further explorations; and again he was sent up the Ottawa. Doubtless, by this time, the "North Sea" of his (Champlain's) imagination had wholly disappeared; for it would be strange indeed if Brulé had not received additional reports concerning the great lake beyond the Mer Douce (Lake Huron), on his last journey. So it was that he, with a companion named Grenolle, now penetrated the region to the northward and northwestward of the Huron country, undertaken, it would seem, in the year 1621, with a full determination to reach the "Grand Lac."

Gabriel Sagard, who records what Brulé told him, did not reach Canada until 1623, going the same year up the Ottawa to the Hurons. Until he had met the interpreter (Brulé), it is certain he had no particular knowledge of Lake Superior or of any copper-mines unless from Indian reports, and in these he would doubtless place little confidence. As an historian, therefore, when writing about what Brulé had told him, he would naturally be cautious, as the relation seemed marvelous, and he had no means of verifying it.

It is true that Sagard does not say, in just so many words, that Brulé reached Lake Superior; but the fact is clearly to be inferred from what he relates. If it was in his mind that the interpreter was only giving him Indian reports, why does he write, making a distinction between such reports and what Brulé declared, as to the length of Lakes Huron and Superior combined?

The savages knew nothing of working copper *ore;* they could only mine pure copper and this was to be found only to the northward of Lake Huron — that is, to the northward of the North Channel, as now called — and farther westward. The ancient manner of obtaining copper from the Lake Superior mines may be gleaned from the following:

"Near the Ontonagon river [Michigan] were discovered in the present century long parallel lines of ancient trenches, which might be traced for miles along the ridges near their summit. These, like others of similar character in other parts of the copper region, were found to mark the outcrop of copper veins, which at some remote period had been worked by an unknown people. The excavations, when cleaned out, were found to reach sometimes twenty feet in depth. They even penetrated under rock cover and left barren places of the vein in the open trenches, the drift forming arches over the drift beneath. Upon the rubbish that had partially filled the pits large trees had grown up. A hemlock standing by the side of a much older stump showed, when cut, over three hundred and fifty distinct annual rings of growth. Buried several feet under its roots, and supported on skids of timber, was a mass of copper that had been worked free from the vein and cleared by fire of all the vein stone that had filled its interstices; ashes and charred wood were found about it; and it was plain that every attempt had been made to reduce its weight, without succeeding in this sufficiently to render its extraction practicable. Its weight proved to be over six tons. The tools of the ancient miners were found in immense numbers, consisting almost exclusively of hammers shaped out of the hard trap rock, with one sharp edge and a groove around them for withing on a handle. The edge of every one was broken, evidently in the service."

While the evidence is not so clear that the two white men reached the extremity of Lake Superior as it is that they went as far as where there were copper mines on the northern shore

APPENDIX.

of Lake Huron (or North Channel, as now known), nevertheless, the presumption is great that their journey westward was not ended until they had entered the mouth of the St. Louis river from the head of the lake. There was surely nothing in the distance traveled to induce a belief that so courageous an explorer as Brulé had already proved himself would be discouraged in urging his canoe so far into an unknown country. It was not so great — so hazardous an undertaking as his exploration of the Susquehanna river and Chesapeake bay. Besides, he and Grenolle were absent two years, which gives them plenty of time to have accomplished the exploration.

Sagard says that, according to *Indian reports*, Lake Huron and Lake Superior combined had a length of "thirty days' journey by canoe," but according to *Brulé's report*, their combined length was "four hundred leagues." Evidently the friar did not look upon Brulé's estimate as an Indian report, but as one made by him after going to the head of the lake last mentioned.

"The Franciscan historian, Sagard, who wrote in 1632, says that Étienne Brulé, the companion of Champlain, left that explorer at Toanche and started with an associate named Grenolle on a voyage to the Upper Lakes. On his return to Quebec, bringing with him a large ingot of copper, he claimed to have visited the Sault, and gave an elaborate description of Lake Superior, but all this information he could have obtained from the Wild Oats [Folles Avoines — Menomonees] of Lake Michigan, who traded with the Algonquins of the North."—*History of the Early Missions in Western Canada.* By Very Rev. W. R. Harris, Dean of St. Catherines. Toronto: 1893. p. 94*n*. It is safe to say, however, had Brulé got his information of that or any other nation of Indians, he would have so stated.

"If Sagard's account is to be trusted, Brulé had in some manner also [that is, in addition to his journey to Carantouan] made his way westward, so as to find the shores of Lake Superior. He averred that it took nine days to reach the western extremity of some such water. The stories which he told of a region of copper mines point to this lake, and Sagard says that Brulé showed to him an ingot of that metal which was found there."— Winsor, in *Cartier to Frontenac*, pp. 121, 122.

[I.] PUBLISHED STATEMENTS OF RECENT WRITERS BEARING DIRECTLY OR
REMOTELY UPON THE QUESTION OF BRULÉ'S
DISCOVERY OF LAKE SUPERIOR.

"Among the pioneers of these wanderers [*voyageurs*] in the American forests was Étienne (Anglicized, Stephen) Brulé, of Champigny. . . . He went with Champlain to the Huron villages near Georgian bay, but did not with his Superior cross Lake Ontario. After three years of roaming, he came back to Montreal, and told Champlain that he had found a river which he descended until it flowed into a sea,— the river by some supposed to be the Susquehanna, and the sea Chesapeake bay. While in this declaration he may have depended upon his imagination, yet to him belongs the undisputed honor of being the first white man to give the world a knowledge of the region beyond Lake Huron.

"Sagard mentions that this bold *voyageur*, with a Frenchman named Grenolle, made a long journey, and returned with a 'lingot' of red copper and with a description of Lake Superior which defined it as very large, requiring nine days to reach its upper extremity, and discharging itself into Lake Huron by a fall."— Rev. Edward D. Neill, A.B., in *Narrative and Critical History of America*, vol. IV, p. 165. (For Sagard's words in French, see Note XXII [b] of this Appendix.)

"The original [of Champlain's map of 1632] was published in the year of its date, but it had been completed before Champlain left Quebec in 1629. The reader will bear in mind that it was made from Champlain's personal explorations and from such other information as could be obtained from the meagre sources which existed at that early period, and not from any accurate or scientific surveys. The information which he obtained from others was derived from more or less doubtful sources, coming as it did from fishermen, fur-traders, and the native inhabitants. The two former undoubtedly constructed, from time to time, rude maps of the coast for their own use. From these, Champlain probably obtained valuable hints, and he was thus able to supplement his own knowledge of the regions with which he was least familiar on the Atlantic coast and in the Gulf of St. Lawrence. *Beyond the limits of his personal explorations on the West, his information was wholly derived from the savages. No European had penetrated into those regions, if we except his servant, Étienne Brûlé, whose descriptions could have been of very little service.* The deficiencies of Champlain's map are here accordingly most apparent. Rivers and lakes farther west than the Georgian bay, and south of it, are sometimes laid down where none exist, and, again, where they do exist, none are portrayed. The outline of Lake Huron, for illustration, was entirely misconceived. A river-like line only of water represents Lake Erie, while Lake Michigan does not appear at all."— Rev. E. F. Slafter, in the *Prince Society Publications of Champlain's*

of Champigny. . . . He went with Champlain to the Huron villages near Georgian bay, but did not with his Superior cross Lake Ontario. After three years of roaming, he came back to Montreal, and told Champlain that he had found a river which he descended until it flowed into a sea,— the river by some supposed to be the Susquehanna, and the sea Chesapeake bay. While in this declaration he may have depended upon his imagination, yet to him belongs the undisputed honor of being the first white man to give the world a knowledge of the region beyond Lake Huron.

"Sagard mentions that this bold *voyageur*, with a Frenchman named Grenolle, made a long journey, and returned with a 'lingot' of red copper and with a description of Lake Superior which defined it as very large, requiring nine days to reach its upper extremity, and discharging itself into Lake Huron by a fall."— Rev. Edward D. Neill, A.B., in *Narrative and Critical History of America*, vol. IV, p. 165. (For Sagard's words in French, see Note XXII [b] of this Appendix.)

"The original [of Champlain's map of 1632] was published in the year of its date, but it had been completed before Champlain left Quebec in 1629. The reader will bear in mind that it was made from Champlain's personal explorations and from such other information as could be obtained from the meagre sources which existed at that early period, and not from any accurate or scientific surveys. The information which he obtained from others was derived from more or less doubtful sources, coming as it did from fishermen, fur-traders, and the native inhabitants. The two former undoubtedly constructed, from time to time, rude maps of the coast for their own use. From these, Champlain probably obtained valuable hints, and he was thus able to supplement his own knowledge of the regions with which he was least familiar on the Atlantic coast and in the Gulf of St. Lawrence. *Beyond the limits of his personal explorations on the West, his information was wholly derived from the savages. No European had penetrated into those regions, if we except his servant, Étienne Brûlé, whose descriptions could have been of very little service.* The deficiencies of Champlain's map are here accordingly most apparent. Rivers and lakes farther west than the Georgian bay, and south of it, are sometimes laid down where none exist, and, again, where they do exist, none are portrayed. The outline of Lake Huron, for illustration, was entirely misconceived. A river-like line only of water represents Lake Erie, while Lake Michigan does not appear at all."— Rev. E. F. Slafter, in the *Prince Society Publications of Champlain's*

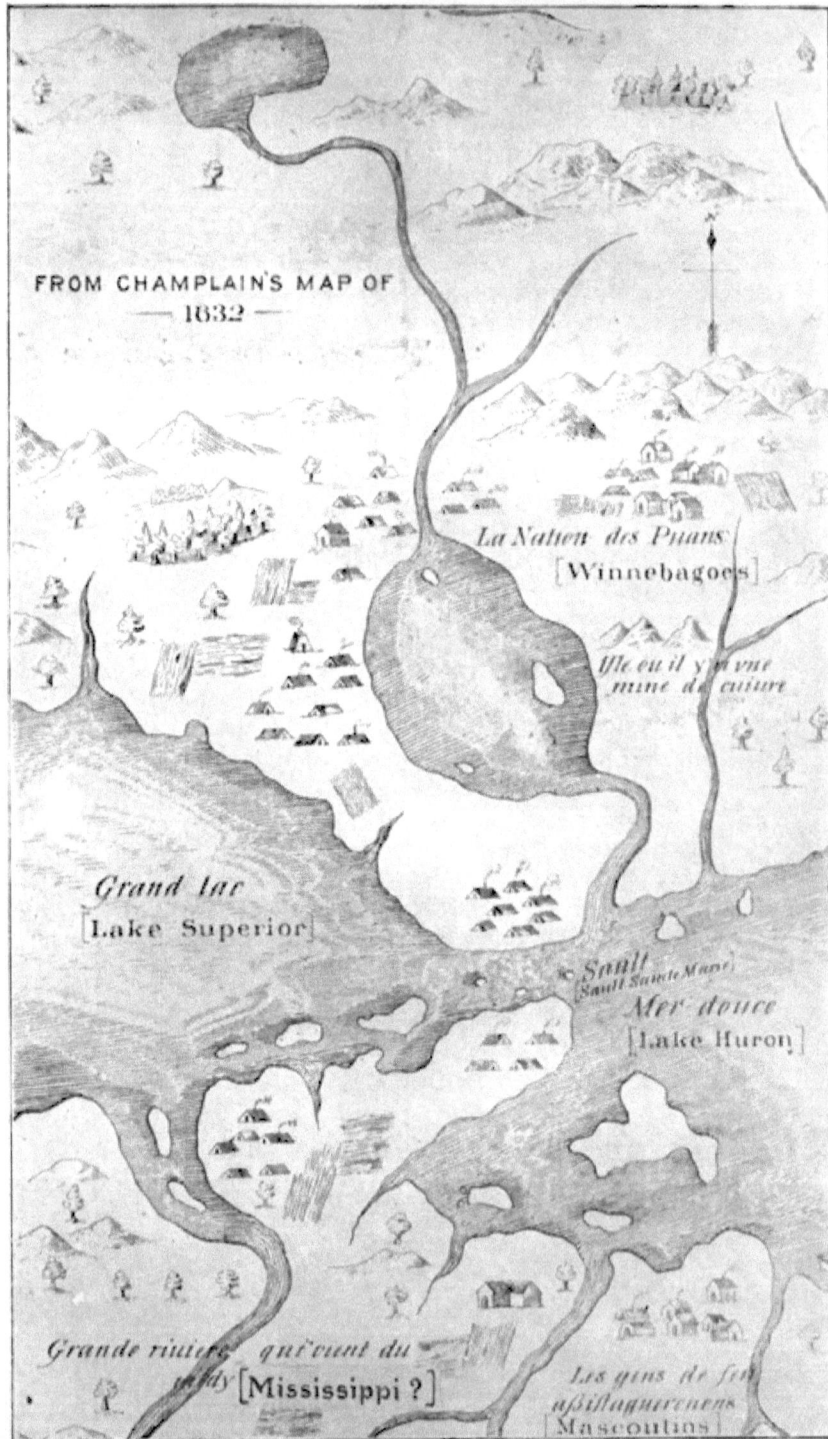

"*Voyages,*" vol. I, pp. 210, 211. (The italicising in the above extract is mine.)*

In the Index to Champlain's map of 1632 is this note: "33 *Riuière des Puans*, coming from a lake where there is a mine of pure red copper." Commenting on this, Mr. Slafter says: "Champlain had not been in this region, and consequently obtained his information from the savages. There is no such lake as he represents on his map and the island producing pure copper may have been Isle Royale in Lake Superior."

The outlet of Lake Superior (with the rapids, or falls) is thus spoken of in the Index to the map mentioned in the preceding paragraph:

"*Sault de Gaston*, nearly two leagues broad, and discharging into the *Mer Douce* [Lake Huron]. It comes from another very large lake, which, with the *Mer Douce*, has an extent of thirty days' journey by canoe, according to the report of the savages." As to the delineations on the map itself, of the vicinity, Winsor (*Cartier to Frontenac*, p. 144) says: "Very curiously there seems to be [on the map] the beginning of the Straits of Mackinaw, with its island nearly in the proper place, while the inlet which stands for Green bay amid the country of the Puants [Winnebagoes] is thrown over to the north side of [Lake] Huron."† Preceding this, Mr. Winsor writes also concerning the map and Index just alluded to:

"In the large map [of 1632] there is perhaps some, but less reason to suspect an alien hand [than in his '*Voyages*' of that year, to which the map is appended]. We get from it the first

---

*Upon Champlain's arrival in London as a prisoner, in 1629, he laid before the French ambassador a map of the country, believed to have been his large map [1632] of New France (see Slafter's "Memoir of Champlain," vol. I, p. 173, of the *Prince Society Publications*).

† We are now satisfied that the lake represented on Champlain's map of 1632, but drawn in the year 1629, having an island where there is a copper mine, is Lake Winnebago, and that the stream leading from it is what is now known as Fox river, but the island should have been represented as being in Lake Superior ; and the lake and river, instead of being to the north of Lake Huron, should have been given as west of Lake Michigan. As Champlain probably received information from Indian reports as to the existence of Lake Winnebago and Fox river, and from Brulé concerning Isle Royale—that he (Brulé) reached it on his trip when he found "pure copper" north of Lake Huron; and as he (Champlain) recollected, though erroneously, that the mine was in Lake Winnebago (as now called), it is not difficult to see why the lake last mentioned should have been placed where it is to be found on the map. It is the fact of Champlain having received knowledge of the existence of a mine of "pure copper" *on an island*, which induces the belief that Isle Royale was visited by Brulé and Grenolle. It is suggested that the island mentioned by Winsor as being "Mackinaw" island is, rather, the Great Manitoulin.

cartographical intimation of a great lake beyond the *Mer Douce* [Lake Huron]. In an explanatory legend, Champlain says that the Saut du Gaston, commemorating a brother of Louis XIII, was near two leagues in width,—it represents the present Sault Ste. Marie,—with its waters coming from a very large lake beyond."

[II.] COMMENTS ON THE PREVIOUS EXTRACTS RELATING TO BRULÉ'S DISCOVERY OF LAKE SUPERIOR:

The language of Neill that to Brulé "belongs the undisputed honor of being the first white man to give to the world a knowledge of the region beyond Lake Huron, is, of course, with little significance, until there is coupled with it the further information that he returned from his "long journey" "with a 'lingot' of red copper and with a description of Lake Superior." That author, notwithstanding his declaration that Brulé took a "long journey," only commits himself to the fact that he afterwards gave to "the world a knowledge of the region" where was to be found pure copper and where existed the great lake; he is cautious to avoid any declaration as to whether, in his judgment, the "bold *voyageur*" visited this the largest body of fresh water on the globe, or the mines whence came the "'lingot' of red copper." Subsequently (*Mag. Western Hist.*, vol. VII, p. 412), he has not the courage of his convictions; for he asserts, in effect, that Brulé did not visit Lake Superior: "There is no evidence that any European, before Anno Domini 1659, explored the shores of Lake Superior. It is true that Indians visiting Quebec had alluded to the big waters in the far west, and Grenolle, one of Champlain's daring men, after an absence of three years, returned from his roaming with a nugget of copper and the description of a lake which required the Indians to paddle their canoes nine days to pass from the eastern to [the] western extremity. More than ten years later, A. D. 1634, the Sieur Nicolet, an interpreter of a trading company, was the first European to spend the winter near the Green bay of Lake Michigan, but he did not pass beyond the Sault du Gaston, now called the Sault Sainte Marie."

As to the declaration of Harris that Sagard says that Brulé left Champlain "at Toanché and started with an associate named Grenolle on a voyage to the Upper Lakes," it may be said that Sagard, in so declaring, is in error; for Champlain himself says he did not part with his interpreter at Toanché, but after he had left that Indian town; and that when he took leave of his patron it was not to go "to the Upper Lakes," but to the

Carantouannais; and that he never after saw Champlain in the Huron country. Harris infers, however, from Sagard's words, that Brulé, on his return from his "voyage to the Upper Lakes," bringing with him a large ingot of copper, "claimed to have visited the Sault [Ste. Marie]," and that he "gave an elaborate description of Lake Superior." That writer is not entirely satisfied but that Brulé might have claimed more credit than he was entitled to; for he adds, as we have seen:— "but all this information he [Brulé] could have obtained from the Wild Oats [Folles Avoines— Menomonees— who lived on the north side of Green bay, in the present Wisconsin] of Lake Michigan, who traded with the Algonquins of the North." However, there is no evidence that Champlain's interpreter met any of the Wild Oats on his journey; and I have been unable to find any account of their having traded with the Beaver nation or with the Oumisagai previous to Brulé's death in 1632, or with any savages living to the southeast of the mouth of French river, although it is highly probable that such may have been the fact previously, but now they were at war with each other.*

The conclusions of Winsor, that, if Sagard's account is to be trusted, "Brulé had in some manner . . . made his way westward so as to find the shores of Lake Superior," rest, of course, wholly upon the credibility of the Franciscan historian. That Sagard's account is to be relied upon is altogether certain. What possible reason could he have had for inventing such an account, or for misstating Brulé's words? None, certainly. Besides, he repeats the story of the visit, so far as Grenolle is concerned; and it is abundantly evident that there was a Frenchman of that name among the Hurons. The good friar's words are: "The interpreter Brulé assured us that beyond the 'Freshwater Sea' [*Mer Douce*— Lake Huron] there was another very large lake, which empties into it by a waterfall." He does not say Brulé assured him that, *from Indian reports*, there " was another very large lake," etc. The map of Champlain of 1632 shows distinctly the position of the strait leading out of Lake Superior, the rapids in the strait, and the Great Manitoulin island. Champlain evidently had had these marked out for him by some one who had been there; and that it was not an Indian is evident from the confidence placed in the relation by the rapids being named, "Sault de Gaston." This surely would not have been done had

---

* At least, such is the inference from what Champlain says. And it is known that the Indians west of Lake Michigan were constantly making war upon those dwelling upon the coast of the North Channel and of the Georgian bay. (See *History of the Discovery of the Northwest, by John Nicolet, in* 1634, passim.)

a knowledge of the existence of the falls rested solely upon Indian reports; a white man (or white men) must have seen them or they would not have been named at all,— surely not in honor of a brother of the King of France.

Slafter's language regarding explorations made previous to 1629, "on the west"— beyond the limits of Champlain's journeyings in that direction — is, as we have seen, that "no European had penetrated into those regions, if we except his [Champlain's] servant, Étienne Brûlé, whose descriptions could have been of little service." But the reason given why they had very little value is not clearly set forth. He urges that, as Champlain had to rely upon Indian reports and upon Brulé's not very serviceable descriptions, of the region "on the west" outside of what he himself had seen, his map published in 1632 is, as to that country, particularly deficient. But these "deficiencies" are only of a serious character where, it is clear, neither Champlain nor Brulé had journeyed.

As the journey of Brulé and Grenolle to Lake Superior occurred after the publication of 1619, of Champlain's *Voyages*, the account of it could not, of course, have found a place in any of his works preceding that date. That no mention is made of it in the edition of 1632 was either the work of an "alien hand" or of Champlain himself, because his interpreter went over to the English at the period of the surrender of Quebec to the latter. What gives color to the belief that the Governor had nothing to do with the omission is the circumstance that, in the Index to the map of 1632 (which accompanies that edition), where Lake Superior is spoken of, almost the exact words employed by Sagard are used,— *stopping short, however, of what the latter says as to Brulé.* Says the Index: "It [the river forming the 'Sault de Gaston'] comes from another very large lake, which, with the Mer Douce, [Lake Huron] has an extent of thirty days' journey by canoe, according to the report of the savages." But thus Sagard: "Which lake [Superior] with the Mer Douce have almost thirty days' journey by canoe in length, according to the account of the savages, *and according to the interpreter* [Brulé] *four hundred leagues in length* [the italicising is ours]." Now, as this Index was not made by Champlain, it becomes highly probable that the omission of the words in italics was not his work. And the same reason which caused the omission of the journey to Lake Superior may have caused the leaving out of the narrative his visit to the Carantouannais. (See Note XVII of this Appendix.)* And this comparison shows conclusively,

* The reasons for these omissions are to be found, in all probability, in

even assuming that Champlain wrote the Index, that what Brulé told him of his journey to Lake Superior corresponded largely with what he had previously told Sagard concerning it.

NOTE XIX.

THE NEUTRAL NATION.

The first white man to gain a knowledge of the existence of the Neutral nation was Champlain in 1616, while on his visit to the Cheveux Relevés:

"They [the Cheveux Relevés] gave us good cheer and welcomed us very cordially, earnestly begging me to assist them against their enemies, who dwell on the banks of the Mer Douce, two hundred leagues distant.

"There is also, at a distance of a two days' journey from them [the Cheveux Relevés], in a southerly direction, another savage nation that produces a large amount of tobacco. This nation is called the Neutrals. They number four thousand warriors, and dwell westward of the Lake of the Entouhonorons [Ontario], which is from eighty to a hundred leagues in extent. They, however, assist the Cheveux Relevés against the Gens de Feu [Mascoutins]. But with the Iroquois and our allies [the Hurons] they are at peace, and preserve a neutrality. There is a cordial understanding towards both of these nations, and they do not venture to engage in any dispute or quarrel, but on the contrary often eat and drink with them like good friends."

The visit of La Roche Daillon to the Neutrals brought to light many facts concerning them. What Brulé had narrated previously relative to the nation can only be conjectured — only that he gave, what Daillon confirmed, a "grand account." "At last," says the friar, "ten men of the last village called 'Ouaroronon, one day's journey from the Iroquois, their relatives and friends, coming to trade at our village [Ounontisaston] came to visit me, and invited me to come and see them, in their village."

Such are the words of Daillon. Now, the phrase "last village" means undoubtedly the "last village" of the Neutrals, on the east towards the Iroquois, not the "last village" visited by Daillon (as generally supposed) before the ten savages made their appearance in the town where he was then sojourning. This is proved by the fact that the savage visitors invited him

what is stated by Kingsford in his *History of Canada*,— that they were made to "influence opinion, so that Canada, restored to France, should be given over entirely to the Jesuits." The latter would be slow to acknowledge the discoveries and explorations of Brulé therefore, as these would militate against their scheme. (See Note I of this Appendix.)

"to come and see them in their village," which, of course, they would not have done had he just left it. As these ten savages went to the town where Daillon was stopping for the purpose of trade, it is altogether certain that he had traveled a considerable distance westward before reaching Ounontisaston. The ten Indians then fell upon the friar and came near killing him; then they robbed him of his goods; but, subsequently, they sent back most of the articles.

Now, as Daillon had not previously visited Ouaroronon, it is quite sure, after this experience, he would not venture there. It is clear then he did not reach the Niagara river from the west, the mouth of which he fondly hoped to discover before leaving the country, so as to bring the Neutrals to trade by way of Lake Ontario with the French on the St. Lawrence.

But there was good reason why Daillon would not make the journey eastward to the Niagara, even if he had known the way and could have gone unattended. He would not wish to provoke the Neutrals to desperation, who, he well knew, were opposed to trading with the French upon the St. Lawrence. Huron jealousy was all-powerful on the north, and Iroquois hatred of the French on the east. The nation would be slow to incur the hatred of either; much slower to bring upon themselves the hostility of both.

The following, then, by Shea (Winsor's *Narrative and Critical History of America*, vol. IV, p. 279), is error: "The Recollect Joseph de la Roche d' Allion [frequently so written] had already in early days [referring to the years 1626 and 1627] crossed the Niagara from the west."

Says Daillon: "Passing the Petun nation, I made acquaintance and friendship with an Indian chief, who is in great credit, who promised to guide me to the Neutral nation and supply Indians to carry our baggage and what little provision we had. . . . He fulfilled what he had promised to our satisfaction, and we slept only five nights in the woods, and on the sixth day arrived at the first village [of the Neutrals], where we were well received, thanks to our Lord, and then at four other villages, which envied each other in bringing us food,— some venison, others squashes, neinthaony, and the best they had."

Daillon says the nation has twenty-eight towns, cities and villages, made like those in the Huron country, and also several little hamlets of seven or eight cabins, built in various parts convenient for fishing, hunting, or agriculture.*

* Harris's *Early Missions in Western Canada*, p. 50.

Thirty-six villages of the Neutrals, according to a recent writer, were in what is now Canadian territory; and the last of the four or five towns on the American side of the Niagara river eastward was where the city of Lockport now stands.*

NOTE XX.
AS TO BRULÉ GOING OVER TO THE ENGLISH.

It is, seemingly, very evident that the invective indulged in against Brulé, as found in the edition of his works of 1632, was written not by Champlain but by the compiler of that book. The words betray a vindictive and revengeful spirit,—charging, as they do, viciousness and licentiousness—which Champlain surely could not have written; for the latter was the very person who had from the beginning urged and supported his young friend in leaving civilization to become thoroughly imbued with Indian life. The words themselves show that they must have been written by an alien hand: "It was a very bad example to send persons of such bad morals as the interpreter Brulé among the Indians, who received a salary of one hundred pistoles a year to urge the savages to trade with us. Such characters ought to have been severely chastised; for it was recognized that that man was vicious and licentious: but what will not be the mischief wrought by the hope of gain, which comes before every other consideration?" †

Such are the words we are asked to believe emanated from Champlain concerning his faithful interpreter, Brulé, because he went over to the British when Kirk made his second appearance in the St. Lawrence. Whether it was really heartless for Brulé to assist in getting the ships up the river may be judged of by the following:

" He [an Indian] had just discovered three ships sailing up the south channel of Orleans. Champlain was alone. All his followers were absent, fishing or searching for roots. At about ten o'clock his servant appeared with four small bags of roots, and the tidings that he had seen . . . three ships a league off,

---

* Id., p. 120. See, further, as to the Neutral nation, Marshall's *The Niagara Frontier*, pp. 5-7; Parkman's *Jesuits of North America*, pp. XLIV, XLV, and the authorities there cited.

† " Le truchement Bruslé à qui l'on donnoit cent pistolles par an, pour inciter les Sauuages à venir à la traitte, ce qui estoit de tres-mauuais exemple, d'enuoyer ainsi des personnes si maluluans, que l'on eust deub chastier seuerement, car l'on recognoissoit cet homme pour estre fort vicieux, & adonné aux femmes ; mais que ne fait faire l'esperance du gain, qui passe par dessus toutes considerations."

behind Point Levi. As man after man hastened in, Champlain ordered the starved and ragged band, sixteen in all, to their posts, whence, with hungry eyes, they watched the English vessels anchoring in the basin below."—Parkman's *Pioneers*, p. 406.

Says Mr. Sulte: "Champlain was very angry at the desertion of the four Frenchmen, Brulé, Baillif, Marsolet and Raye, to the English. No doubt that, in accordance with the barbarous customs of the XVIth and XVIIth centuries, the four deserved hanging; but they were not soldiers: they had the right to look anywhere for a living; and if the question of patriotism comes in, I would like to know where it existed in France, when so many noble warriors made a business of enlisting in foreign armies against France. Patriotism was created one hundred years ago by the French Revolution.

"Even now, considering the extraordinary circumstances of Quebec, in 1629, if such a situation was to present itself to us, we would drop all patriotism for a loaf of bread, especially when hired as common laborers and not engaged as soldiers."

NOTE XXI.

CANNIBALISM AMONG THE HURONS.

Cannibalism, except to a limited extent, was not practiced by the Indians of North America at and after the discovery of the New World by Columbus; at least, the eating of human flesh was only to gratify their appetites upon rare occasions and was then restricted to the devouring of the bodies of enemies. It was an act of revenge and carried with it, also, something of an idea of a religious rite. Just what nations were addicted to it can not be stated; although it is known to have been indulged in by those of the Iroquois and Algonquin families. The Hurons sometimes ate a foe they had killed (see *Relation des Hurons*, 1636, p. 121; 1637, p. 118); so, too, the Miamis.

"I saw the Iroquois," writes Father Bressani, "tear out the heart from a Huron captive whom they had killed, and in the presence of the other prisoners roast and devour it." "In a word," says Lalemant, "they eat human flesh with as much appetite and more relish than hunters eat the meat of the deer." It was, however, an appetite promoted, mostly, by the spirit of revenge.

NOTE XXII.

EXTRACTS FROM SAGARD'S "HISTOIRE DU CANADA" (PARIS EDITION, 1866) RELATING TO BRULÉ.

[a]

"L'un de nos François nommé Crenole [Grenolle], ayant esté a la traicte du coste nord, en une nation esloignée environ 100 lieuës des Hurons, tirant à la mine cuivre, nous dit à son retour y avoir veu plusieurs filles ausquelles on avoit couppé le bout du nés selon la coustume du païs, pour avoir faict bresche à leur honneur."— p. 328.

[Translation.]

One of our Frenchmen named Crenole [Grenolle], having been on the journey of the north shore to a nation about 100 leagues distant from the Hurons, approaching the copper mine, told us on his return that he had seen there several girls the end of whose noses had been cut off, in accordance with the custom of the country, for having made a breach in their honor.

---

[b]

Il se trouve une autre grande difficulté en ces langues (Huron, Ebiceriny, Montaignais) en la prononciation de quelques syllables, à laquelle consistent les diverses signification d'un mesme mot qui est une difficulté plus grande que l'on ne pense pas, car manquez seulement en une vous manquez en tout, ou si vous vous faites entendre, ce sera tout autrement que vous ne desirez, comme en ce mot Ebicerinyen: Kidauskinne, lequel avec une certaine façon de prononcer veut dire, tu n'as point d'esprit, et par un autre ton signifie: tu as menty. Ainsi en est-il de quantité d'autres mots, c'est pourquoi il faut ayder à la lettre, et apprendre la cadence si on y veut profiter, car le Truchement Bruslé s'y est quelquefois lui-mesme trouvé bien empesché et moi-encore plus. . . . p. 338.

[Translation.]

There is another great difficulty in these languages (Huron, Ebiceriny, Montaignais) in the pronunciation of some of the syllables, in which consists the different significations of the same word, which is a greater difficulty than one would think, for if you fail only in one you fail in all, or if you make yourself understood, it may be quite otherwise than you desire; as in this

Ebicerinyen word, Kidauskinne; which, pronounced in a certain manner, signifies, "you have no sense;" and, with another accent, signifies, "you have lied." It is thus with a quantity of other words, which is the reason it is necessary to aid the spelling, and learn the cadence if you wish to avail yourself of them, for the Interpreter Brulé sometimes found himself much embarrassed with them and I myself still more. . . .

---

[c]

Ce pauvre Bruslé, quoy qu'assez sçavant dans le païs des Hurons et lieux circonvoisins, se perdit neantmoins et s'égara de telle sorte que faute d'avoir une de ses bousoles, ou prins garde au soleil, il tourna le dos aux Hurons, traversa force païs et coucha quelques nuicts dans les bois, jusques à un matin qu'ayant trouvé un sentier battu, il se rendit par icelui dans un village d'Hiroquois, où il fut à peine arrivé qu'il fut saisi et constitué prisonnier en ensuite condamné à la mort par le conseil des Sages.

Le pauvre homme bien estonné ne sçavait à quel Sainct se voüer, car d'esperer misericorde il scavait bien qu'il n'estoit point en lieu, il eut dont [sc. donc] recours à Dieu et à la patience, et se soubmit à ses divines volontez, plus par force qu'autrement, car il n'estoit guere devot, tesmoin ce qu'il nous dit un jour, que s'estant trouvé en un autre grand peril de la mort, pour toute priere il dit son Benedicite.

Or je ne sçay s'il le dit icy se voyant prisonnier et dans le premier appareil de la mort, car des-ja ils l'avaient faict coucher de son long contre terre et lui arrachaient la barbe, lorsque l'un d'eux avisant un Agnus Dei, qu'il portait pendu à son col, lui voulant arracher, il se prit à crier et dit à ses bourreaux, que s'ils lui ostaient, Dieu les en chastierait, comme il fist; car ils n'eurent pas plutost mis la main dessus pour lui tirer du col, que le ciel auparavant serein, se troubla et envoya tant d'esclairs et d'orages et de foudres, qu'ils en creurent estre au dernier jour, s'enfuyrent dans leurs cabanes et laisserent là leur prisonnier, qui se leva et s'enfuit comme les autres mais d'un autre côté. . . .

A la fin ce fortuné Bruslé a este du depuis condamné à la mort, puis mangé par les Hurons, ausquels il avait si longtemps servy de Truchement, et le tout pour une hayne qu'ils conceurent contre luy pour je ne sçay qu'elle faute qu'il commit à leur endroit.

Il y avait beaucoup d'années qu'il demeurait avec eux, vivait quasi comme eux, et servait de Truchement aux Français, et après tout cela n'a remporté pour toute recompense qu'une morte douleureuse et une fin funeste et malheureuse; je prie Dieu qu'il lui fasse misericorde, s'il lui plaist et aye pitié de son ame.— p. 430.

[Translation.]

This poor Brulé, though very well-informed about the country of the Hurons and the surrounding regions, got lost nevertheless and strayed so far from lack of having one of his compasses, or taking notice of the sun, that he turned his back on the Hurons, traversed many regions and slept several nights in the woods, until one morning having found a beaten path he proceeded by this to a village of the Iroquois, where he had scarcely arrived when he was seized and made prisoner, and then condemned to death by the council of the Sages.

The poor man, much astonished, did not know to which Saint to make vows, for he knew well there was no chance of any hope of mercy, so he had recourse to God and to patience, and submitted himself to his Divine will, more by force than otherwise, for he was not very pious, as witness what he said to us one day, that finding himself in another great peril of death, for all prayer he said his Benedicite.

Now I do not know whether he said it here, seeing himself a prisoner and in solemn preparation for death, for already they had made him lie down at full length on the ground, and were pulling out his beard, when one of them perceiving an Agnus Dei, which he wore hung at his neck, wishing to snatch it from him, he began to cry out and said to his executioners that if they took it from him, God would chastise them, as He did: for they had no sooner put their hands upon him to draw it from his neck, than the sky, before this serene, grew cloudy and sent so many flashes of lightning and tempests, that they believed the last day had come, and fled into their huts leaving their prisoner there, who rose and fled like the others but in another direction. . . .

Finally this fortunate Brulé was later condemned to death and eaten by the Hurons, to whom he had so long served as Interpreter, and all for a hatred which they had conceived against him for I do not know what fault which he had committed with respect to them.

He had dwelt with them a great many years, lived almost as they did, and served as Interpreter to the French, and after all that, he had gained for all recompense only a painful death and a sad and unfortunate end; I pray God to have mercy on him, if it pleases Him, and to have pity on his soul.

---

[d]

Ils m'ont monstré plusieurs rochers sur le chemin de Kebec, ausquels ils croyent presider quelque esprit, et entr'autres, ils me monstrerent un à quelque 150 lieuës de là, qui avoit une profonde caverne de tres-difficile accés. Ils me voulaient persuader et faire croire à toute force avec eux, que ce rocher avait este autrefois homme mortel comme nous et qu'eslevant les bras et les mains en haut, il s'estait metamorphosé en cette pierre et devenu à succession de temps un si puissant rocher, lequels ils ont en veneration et lui offrent du petun en passant par devant avec leurs canots, non toutes les fois, mais quand ils doutent que leur voyage doive reussir; et lui offrant ce petun qu'ils jettent dans l'eau contre la roche même, ils lui disent tien prend courage et fai que nous ayons bon voyage, avec quelques autres paroles que je n'entends point, et le Truchement Bruslé duquel nous avons parlé au chapitre precedant nous dit (à la confusion) d'auoir une fois fait pareille offrande avec eux (de quoy nous le tancâmes fort) et que son voyage lui fut plus profitable qu'aucuns autres qu'il ait jamais faict en tous ces païs-là.— p. 456.

[Translation.]

They showed me several rocks on the road to Quebec, over which they believe some spirit presides, and among others they showed me one at about 150 leagues from there, which had a deep cavern very difficult of access. They wished to persuade me into believing absolutely with them that this rock had been formerly a mortal man like us, and that raising his arms and hands on high he had been transformed into this stone and become in the course of time so powerful a rock, which they hold in veneration and offer to it tobacco in passing before it with their canoes, not every time, but when they are doubtful of their voyage being successful; and when offering this tobacco which they throw into the water against the rock itself, they say to it: Hear! Take courage and give us a good voyage, with some other words which I do not understand, and the Interpreter Brulé, of whom we spoke in the preceding chapter, told us (to our confusion) that he once made a similar offering with them (for which we rebuked him severely) and that his voyage was more profitable to him than any others which he had ever made in all these regions.

[e]

Le Truchement Bruslé avec quelques Sauvages nous ont asseuré qu'au delà de la mer douce, il y a un autre grandissime lac, qui se descharge dans icelle par une cheute d'eau que l'on a surnommé le Saut de Gaston, ayant près de deux lieuës de large, lequel lac avec la mer douce contiennent environ trente journées de canots selon le rapport des Sauvages et du truchement quatre cent lieuës de longueur.—p. 589.

[Translation.]

The Interpreter Bruslé with some Savages assured us that beyond the fresh sea there is another very large lake, which empties into this one by a waterfall named the Saut de Gaston, being nearly two leagues wide, which lake with the fresh sea contains about thirty days' journey by canoe according to the statement of the Savages, and of the interpreter four hundred leagues in length.

[f]

Premierement il y a quantité de pelleteries de diverses especes d'animaux terrestres & amphibies, comme vous avez pû remarquer dans le chapitre qui traitte des animaux terrestres & aquatiques. Il y a des mines de cuiure desquelles on pourroit tirer du profit, s'il y avoit du monde & des ouvriers qui a voulussent travailler fidellement, ce qui se pourroit faire, si on y avoit estably des Collonnies: car environ 80. ou 100. lieuës des Hurons, il y a une mine de cuyure rouge, de laquelle le Truchement Bruslé me monstra un lingot au retour d'un voyage qu'il fit à la nation voisine avec un nommé Grenolle.—p. 716.

[Translation.]

In the first place there are a quantity of furs of different species of terrestrial and amphibious animals, as you have been able to observe in the chapter which treats of the terrestrial and aquatic animals. There are copper mines from which much profit might be drawn if there were people and workmen who would be willing to work faithfully, which could be done if colonies were established there: for about 80 or 100 leagues from the Hurons there is a mine of red copper from which the Interpreter Brulé showed me an ingot, on his return from a journey which he made to the neighboring people, with a man named Grenolle.

[g]

De là nous allames cabaner à la petite nation que nos Hurons appellent Queunontateronons — Le Truchement Bruslé, qui s'estant là venu cabaner avec nous, traicta un chien duquel nous fismes festin le lendemain matin en compagnie de quelques François; puis nous partimes encore.— p. 751.

[Translation.]

From there we went to live in huts among the little nation which our Hurons call Queunontateronons. The Interpreter Brulé, who being there, came to live in our hut with us, obtained a dog on which we made a feast on the following morning in company with several Frenchmen; then we set out again.

---

[h]

Nous avions esté fort mal couchez la nuict passée (à Saut S. Louis) mais nous ne fumes pas mieux la suivante, car il nous la fallut passer à deux lieuës du Cap de Victoire, sous un arbre bien peu à couverts des pluyes, qui durerent jusques au dit Cap où desja estoit arrivé depuis deux jours le Truchement Bruslé, avec deux ou trois canots Hurons, duquel j'appris la deffense que les Montaignais et Algoumequins leur avaient faites de passer outre, voulant à toute force qu'ils attendissent là avec eux les barques de la traicte, et qu'ayant pensé leur resister ils s'estaient mis en hazard d'estre tous assommez, particulierement luy Truchement Bruslé qui en avait esté pour son sac à petun et craignait encore un autre plus mauvais party, s'y on n'y apportait quelque remède.

Je trouvai ce procédé fort mauvais et en fis quelques reproches à ces mutins, qui me dirent pour excuse que si personne ne descendait, les barques seraient contrainctes de les venir trouver, sans avoir la peine de trainer leurs femmes et leurs enfants jusques à Kebec, où il n'y avait de quoy disner pour eux. Je leur dis que j'y avais necessairement affaire et que je desirais y descendre que pour eux qu'ils en fissent comme ils voudroient. Cette resolution ne les contenta pas beaucoup, neantmoins ils ne voulurent pas me violenter comme ils avaient faict le Truchement, mais ils trouverent une autre invention plus favorable pour intimider nos Hurons et tirer d'eux quelque petit present.

Ils firent donc semer un faux bruit qu'ils venoient de recevoir vingt colliers de pourcelaine des Ignierhonons (ennemis mortels des Hurons) à la charge de les envoyer advertir à l'instant de l'arrivée desdits Hurons, pour les venir tous mettre à mort et qu'en bref ils seraient icy.

Nos gens vainement espouventez de cette mauvaise nouvelle tindrent conseil là-dessus, un peu à l'écart dans le bois où je fus appellé avec le Truchement, qui estait d'aussi legère croyance qu'eux et cotizerent tous, qui de rets, qui de petun, farine et autres choses, qu'ils donnerent aux capitaines des Montagnais et Algoumequins pour estre protegez contre leurs ennemis. . . .

Pour suivre le dessein que j'avais de partir du Cap de Victoire pour Kebec, nonobstant la contradiction de nos Algoumequins et Montagnais, je fis jetter notre canot en l'eau dès le lendemain de grand matin, que tout le monde dormoit encore et n'esveillay que le Truchement pour me suivre, . . . p. 752.

[Translation.]

We had had a very bad sleeping place the past night (at Saut S. Louis) but we were not better off the following, for we had to pass it within two leagues of Cape Victory, under a tree very little sheltered from the rains which lasted up to the said Cape, where already the Interpreter Brulé had arrived two days before with two or three Huron canoes, from whom I learned that the Montaignais and Algoumequins had forbidden them to pass beyond, desiring at all costs that they would await there with them the boats for the journey, and that having thought of resisting them they had put themselves in danger of all being killed, particularly the Interpreter Brulé who had been in danger on account of his bag of tobacco, and who feared a still worse condition, if some remedy were not applied.

I found this proceeding very bad, and made some reproaches to these mutineers, who said to me in excuse that if no one descended, the boats would be forced to come to find them, without their having the trouble of dragging their wives and children to Quebec where there was nothing for them to eat. I told them that I had business there and desired to descend, and that for them they could do as they wished. This resolution did not much content them, nevertheless they did not wish to do violence to me as they had done to the Interpreter, but they found another contrivance more favorable for intimidating our Hurons and getting from them some little gift.

They caused a false report to be spread that they had just received twenty porcelain necklaces from the Ignierhonons, (mortal enemies of the Hurons), on condition that they would send to inform them immediately of the arrival of the said Hurons, that they might come to put them all to death, and that in short they would be here.

Our people, uselessly terrified by this bad news, held council thereupon a little apart in the woods, where I was called with the Interpreter, who was as ready of belief as they, and they assessed all, nets, tobacco, flour and other things, which they gave to the captains of the Montagnais and Algoumequins to be protected against their enemies. . . .

In order to follow out the plan which I had of departing from Cape Victory for Quebec, notwithstanding the opposition of our Algoumequins and Montagnais, I had our canoe thrown down into the water very early the next day while everybody was still asleep, and awakened only the Interpreter to follow me. . . .

INDEX.

Accomack Indians, 84.
"Adoresetoüy," Seneca name for the French, 91.
Algonquins, 10, 13, 16, 26, 28, 33, 44, 85, 104, 122, 127, 140, 161, 166.
Algoumequins (Algonquins), 173, 174.
Allumette Island, 27, 129.
Amantacha, a Huron, 119, 122.
Andastes, 149, 153.
Anthropological Society of Washington, D. C., 148.
Antouhonorons (Onondagas), 38, 59.
Atchiligoüian Indians, 105.
Atlantic Ocean, 81, 85.
Attigouautans (Hurons), 32, 132, 133.
"Atinouaentans," 95.
Attiwandaronks (Neuter Nation), 148.
Attiwandarons (Neutrals), 50, 60, 111.
"Axacan," 69.

Baillif, 166.
Beaver Indians, 105, 106, 155.
Block, Adrian, 77.
Brébeuf, John de, 110, 112, 114, 123.
Bref Récit (Cartier's) gives particulars of ulterior regions, 101, 102.
Bressani, Father, 166.
BRULÉ, STEPHEN, born about 1592, in Champigny, France, 12; came to New France in 1608, with Champlain, *ibid.*; was one of Quebec's original inhabitants, 13; taken, in 1610, up the St. Lawrence, by Champlain, *ibid.*; was probably in the battle of June 19th (see *frontispiece*), when the Iroquois were defeated, 14; seized with a desire to go with the Hurons to their country, *ibid.*; starts upon his journey, 18; returns the next year (1611) to the St. Lawrence, 19; meets Champlain at Lachine rapids, *ibid.*; relates to him what he had seen in the Huron country, 20; was the first European to visit Lake Huron, *ibid.*; made the first exploration of the Province of Ontario, 21; acts for the first time as interpreter for Indians, 22; was the first white person to descend Lachine rapids, 24; lives, probably, from July, 1611, to July, 1615, among Algonquins, 25; accompanying Champlain and, acting as his interpreter, he again goes to the Huron country, 31 *et seq.*; permitted by Champlain to go to the country of the Carantouannais with twelve

Indians of that nation, 43; starts, Sept. 8th, for Carantouan, their principal village, 47; his journey thither, 49 *et seq.;* on his way assists his savage companions to attack and defeat a party of Senecas, 52; reaches Carantouan, on the upper waters of the Susquehanna, in safety, 52; was the first white person to traverse any portion of Western New York, *ibid.;* welcomed with great joy at Carantouan, 53; goes, with five hundred Carantouannais, to the Onondaga country to assist Champlain and the Hurons, 54; reaches the vicinity of the Onondaga stronghold too late to aid them, 63; returns with the Carantouannais to Carantouan, *ibid.;* explores, in the winter of 1615–16, the Susquehanna and Chesapeake country to the ocean, 65 *et seq.;* returns in the spring of 1616 to Carantouan, 86; was the first European to explore what is now Pennsylvania, *ibid.;* starts with five or six Carantouannais for the Huron villages, 87; is attacked by Seneca Indians and runs for his life, *ibid.;* hopelessly and alone, he wanders about, 88; in danger of starvation, he surrenders to three Senecas, 89; is led to their village and questioned, 91; is terribly scourged, *ibid.;* is astonishingly delivered from torture by the coming on of a thunderstorm, 92; is unbound by a Seneca chief and treated kindly, 93; again starts for the Huron villages, this time escorted four days on his way by Senecas, ·94; reaches the Huron villages and finds that Champlain had started back to the St. Lawrence, 95; rests for a considerable time with his Huron friends, *ibid.;* returns, in the summer of 1618, to the St. Lawrence, and on July 7th meets Champlain at Three Rivers, 96; relates to his patron all the circumstances of his journey to Carantouan and the Atlantic ocean, and gives him the particulars of his return, *ibid.;* is urged by Champlain to undertake further explorations, 97; consents to go again to the Western wilderness, *ibid.;* turns his canoe to the northward after reaching the Georgian bay of Lake Huron, 99; proceeding as far as the North Channel, he rests among the Beaver Indians for the winter, 100; returns, in the summer of 1620, to the St. Lawrence, *ibid.;* proceeds to the Huron country in 1621, and, with one Grenolle, goes to the northward, *ibid.;* reaches the " Sault de Ste. Marie," 106; finds, there, ancestors of the present Chippewas, 107; discovers Lake Superior, 107 *et seq.;* goes, probably, along its north shore to the head of the lake, 108; visits Isle

Royale in returning, *ibid.;* after reaching Quebec in July, 1623, he again journeys to the Huron country, but accompanies, the next year, some Hurons to the St. Lawrence, *ibid.;* goes back, in 1625, to the homes of those savages, 110; makes an exploring tour thence to the Neutral nation, 111; remains there until the next spring, 112; returns to the St. Lawrence the same year, *ibid.;* in 1627, again visits the Hurons in their villages, returning the next year to Quebec, 117; acts as pilot for the English vessels when, in 1629, Quebec surrendered to Kirk, 118; again journeys (and for the last time) to the Huron country, 119; gave himself, upon his arrival there, wholly to savage life, 120; in 1632, was killed, at Toanché, by the Hurons and eaten by them, *ibid.;* his death causes, subsequently, great terror to the Hurons, 123; critical notes on his discoveries, explorations and adventures, 128, 129, 130, 131, 138, 139, 140, 141, 142, 147, 150, 151, 152, 153, 154, 155, 156, 157, 158, 159, 160, 161, 162, 165, 166.

Cabot, John, in 1797, reaches the North American continent, 1.
Cabot, Sebastian, explores eastern coast of North America in 1798, from Labrador to Virginia, 1.

Cahiagué, a Huron town, 34, 35, 59, 90, 133.
Cannibalism among the Hurons, 120; in North America, 166.
Canningoes (Mohawks), 148.
Carantouannais (Andastes), 22, 37, 38, 39, 40, 41, 42, 43, 48, 51, 52, 53, 54, 56, 58, 63, 64, 65, 68, 79, 81, 82, 85, 87, 88, 90, 132, 136, 141, 148, 150, 152, 153, 162.
Carantouan, chief town of the Carantouannais, 37, 38, 47, 50, 51, 53, 62, 63, 64, 65, 79, 80, 81, 82, 86, 87, 88, 90, 111, 135, 143, 150, 153.
Carantowans (Carantouannais), 148.
Carhagouha, a Huron village, 34.
Cartier, James, 3, 4, 5, 6, 101, 102, 129, 138, 139.
Cartier to Frontenac (Winsor) cited, 6, 21, 59, 62, 104, 107, 119, 126, 128, 135, 138, 140, 141, 143, 157, 159.
"Castle Island," a Dutch trading post, 78.
"Cats" (Eries), 50, 148.
Cayuga Indians, 36, 39, 148.
Champlain, Samuel, sent, in 1603, to the St. Lawrence, 7; his previous history, *ibid.;* ascends the St. Lawrence to Hochelaga (Montreal) island, 8; gains some knowledge of the Great Lakes and Niagara falls, *ibid.;* returns to France, 9; in 1608, sails again for New France, 10; made lieutenant-governor of Canada, *ibid.;* begins the settlement of Quebec, *ibid.;* joins the

Algonquins and Montagnais on an expedition against the Iroquois, and discovers Lake Champlain, 11; defeats the savage enemy, *ibid.;* on June 19th, 1610, with Indian allies, again attacks and defeats the Iroquois, 14; sends Stephen Brulé, his servant, to the Huron country, 15 *et seq.;* sails again (Aug. 18th, 1610) for France, 18; returns in May, 1611, to Canada, *ibid.;* establishes a trading-post on Montreal island, 19; greets Brulé at Lachine rapids on return of the latter from the Hurons, *ibid.;* makes inquiries of the Hurons concerning their country, 22; his policy in sending young men among the savages to become interpreters, 24; in 1611, goes back to France, 26; in 1613, sails for the St. Lawrence, 27; ascends the Ottawa in a vain attempt to discover the North Sea, *ibid.;* having returned to France, he again sets sail, and, on May 15th, 1615, reaches Quebec, 29; goes thence to the country of the Hurons to aid them against the Iroquois, 29 *et seq.;* on the 17th of August, 1615, reaches the principal Huron town, 35; hears of the Carantouannais, allies of the Hurons, 40; learns from some ambassadors of that nation of their country on the upper waters of the Susquehanna, 41; sends Brulé, who had accompanied him to the Hurons, with the ambassadors on their return, 43; instructs Brulé to urge the Carantouannais to move to the assistance of the Hurons, *ibid.;* marches with Huron and other savages against the principal Onondaga village, 44; reaches, early in October, 1615, the Onondaga stronghold and invests it, 46; attacks the Iroquois fort and fails to capture it, 54 *et seq.;* returns with his savages to the Huron country, 59; visits the Tobacco nation, and the Cheveux Relevés, 60; arrives July 11th, 1616, at Quebec, 62; hears of Brulé, his interpreter, before starting for the St. Lawrence, 90; meets Brulé at Three Rivers, July 7th, 1618, and hears the story of the strange adventures of the latter, 96; in 1627, becomes a member of the Company of New France (the "Hundred Associates"), 115; refuses, in 1628, to surrender Quebec to the English, 116; obliged to capitulate the next year, 118; conveyed a prisoner to England, but soon released, *ibid.;* again clothed with authority in Canada, 121; of his published works, 125.

Charioquois (Hurons), 23, 131.
Chaudière (City of Ottawa), 108.
Chesapeake bay, 67, 68, 69, 70, 76, 81, 84, 85, 87, 144, 145, 147, 157, 158.
Cheveux Relevés Indians, 33, 60, 100, 111, 163.

Chippewas, 107.
"Chisapeack" (Chesapeake), bay of, 69.
Chouontouaroüon, identical with the Seneca Indians, 40, 43, 132.
Christiansen, Henry, 77, 78.
Clark, Gen. John S., 132, 135.
Company of New France, 114, 116.
Conestoga creek, 82.
Conestogas, 150.
Conewago Falls, 83, 144, 145.
Conquest of Canada (Warburton) cited, 62, 119.
Copper and copper mines in the Lake Superior region, 5, 15, 102, 103, 130, 155, 156, 158, 159.
Cortereal, Gaspar, voyage of, 1.
Crenole (Grenolle), 106, 167.

Daillon, Joseph de la Roche, a Franciscan priest, 112, 113, 114, 138, 163, 164.
De Caen, Emery, 110, 114, 119.
De Caen, William, 110, 114.
De Chastes (Amyn), 7.
De la Roche, Francis, Lord of Roberval, see Roberval.
Delaware river, 79, 81.
De Monts, Sieur, 9, 15, 18.
De Noue, Jesuit missionary, 112, 114.
Des Sauvages, Champlain's first publication, 125.
Dinondadies (Tobacco nation), 148.
Documents Relating to the Colonial History of the State of New York (O'Callaghan) cited, 79, 130.
"Dotted line" on Champlain's Map of 1632, 40, 143.

Drummond island discovered by Brulé, 105.

Early Chapters of Cayuga History (Hawley) cited, 132.
Early Missions in Western Canada (Harris) cited, 51, 113, 114, 157, 160, 164.
Entouhonorons identical with the Onondagas, 36, 37, 38, 133, 151.
Erie, city of, 143.
Eries, 50, 51, 141, 142, 148, 149.
Evening Journal, The (Ottawa), cited, 16, 18, 52, 129, 153.

Five Nation Indians (Iroquois), 10, 29, 36, 133, 147, 148, 150.
Folles Avoines (Menomonees), 157, 161.
"Fort Nassau," small Dutch post, 78, 79.
"Fresh Sea" (Lake Huron), see Mer Douce.
"Freshwater Sea" (Lake Huron), 140.

Gandastogues (Andastes), 149.
Geddes, George, 135.
Génerall Historie of Virginia (Smith), cited, 71, 84, 142, 144, 145.
Gens de Feu (Mascoutins), 163.
Georgian bay, 20, 32, 33, 49, 62, 85, 96, 99, 104, 138, 158.
"Good Iroquois" (Hurons), 129.
Grand Detour, 51, 76, 143.
"Grand Lac" (Lake Superior), 103, 155.
Genesee river, 90, 94, 148.
Gravé, Francis, see Pontgravé.
Great Manitoulin island, 101, 105, 161.

INDEX

Green bay, 159, 160, 161.
Grenolle, a companion of Brulé, 100, 104, 106, 112, 114, 158, 159, 160, 162.
Guss, Prof. A. L., 38, 73, 82, 84, 145, 146, 148.
Gomez, Stephen, 68.

Harris, Very Rev. W. R., 51, 113, 114, 157, 160, 164.
Hertel, 18, 130.
Histoire de la Nouvelle France (Lescarbot) cited, 137, 139, 142.
Histoire du Canada (History of Canada — Sagard) cited, 26, 91, 92, 106, 107, 121, 167 *et seq*.
History of Canada (Garneau), 114, 140.
History of Canada (Kingsford) cited, 98, 126, 137, 141, 163.
History of Canada (MacMullen) cited, 101.
History of Canada (Smith) cited, 118.
History of the Early Missions in Western Canada (Harris) cited, 51, 113, 114, 157, 160, 164.
History of Maryland (Sharf) cited, 68, 69, 145.
History of New France (Charlevoix — Shea's translation) cited, 118, 126.
Historical Register, The, cited, 38, 69, 73, 83, 84, 146, 148.
History of the City of New York (Lamb) cited, 77, 78.
History of the Discovery of the Northwest, by John Nicolet, in 1634 (Butterfield) cited, 62, 89, 105, 106, 114, 119, 161.

History of the State of New York (Brodhead) cited, 78, 79.
Hochelaga, island of, 4, 101.
Hudson, Henry, 68, 76, 79.
Humber river, 48, 49, 143.
Hundred Associates, 115, 116, 117.
Hurons, 10, 15, 16, 20, 22, 23, 30, 34, 36, 37, 39, 40, 42, 44, 60, 62, 90, 94, 95, 96, 97, 102, 104, 105, 106, 109, 110, 111, 112, 114, 120, 121, 126, 127, 129, 130, 138, 148, 149, 150, 155, 166, 167, 168, 169, 172, 173.
Huron-Iroquois, 129.

Iroquet, an Algonquin Indian chief, 15, 16, 19, 23, 46, 129, 130, 131.
Iroquois, 10, 13, 29, 30, 36, 51, 88, 94, 95, 126, 129, 142, 143, 148, 154, 163.
Isle des Allumettes, 27.
Isle Royale, 108, 159.

Jesuits in North America (Parkman) cited, 132, 143, 165.
Jesuit Relations and Allied Documents (Thwaites) cited, 6, 120.

"Kebec," signification of the word, see "Quebec."
Kingsford, William, 98, 126, 137, 141, 163.
"Kirke," "Kirtk," and other synonyms of Admiral Kirk's name, 116.
Kirk, Lewis, 117.
Kirk, Admiral David, 116, 117, 118.
Kirk, Thomas, 117.

"Kuscarawaocks" (Nanticoke Indians), 84.

Lachine rapids, 6, 8, 19, 23, 24, 27, 100, 131.
Lake Champlain, 129, 140.
Lake Couchiching, 35, 52, 134.
Lake Erie, 5, 8, 50, 76, 140, 143, 148, 158.
Lake Huron, 5, 8, 15, 20, 96, 100, 101, 111, 130, 138, 139, 140, 155, 156, 157, 158, 159.
Lake Michigan, 8, 158, 159, 161.
Lake Nipissing, 20, 26, 32, 44, 62, 100, 127, 130, 140.
Lake of the Entouhonorons (Ontario), 163.
Lake Onondaga, 46, 135.
Lake Ontario, 5, 8, 44, 45, 46, 48, 49, 59, 76, 111, 130, 133, 135, 138, 139, 140, 141, 143, 164.
Lake Simcoe, 48, 49, 52, 62, 63, 129, 133, 134, 138, 140, 143.
Lake St. Clair, 8.
Lake St. Louis (Ontario), 137.
Lake St. Peter, 129, 130, 140.
Lake Superior, 5, 8, 60, 101, 102, 130, 155, 157, 158, 159, 162, 163; discovered by Brulé, 99, 107 *et seq.*, 154 *et seq.*
Lake Two Mountains, 23, 131.
Lake Winnebago, 159.
Lamb, Martha J., 77, 78.
La Salle and the Discovery of the Great West (Parkman) cited, 49.
Lavalée, companion of Grenolle, 112, 113.
Laverdière, C. H., 16, 125, 126.
Le Caron, Father Joseph, 30, 31, 34, 35, 112, 114, 139.
Le Clercq, Récollet writer, 55, 134.

"Little Nation" (Algonquins), 122, 172.
"Louis de Sainte Foi" (Amantacha), 119.

Magazine of American History, The, cited, 126, 135, 136, 137.
Magazine of Western History, The, cited, 160.
Manhattan island, 42, 77, 78.
Map of 1612 (Champlain's), 140.
Map of 1632 (Champlain's), 38, 42, 50, 81, 132, 137, 138, 143, 147, 158, 159.
Map of Virginia (Smith), 71, 145.
Marguerie, 18, 130.
Marshall, O. H., 62, 126, 132, 135, 136, 137, 138.
Margry, Pierre, 126.
Marquez, Pedro Menendez, 69.
Marsolet, Nicholas, 18, 118, 130, 152, 166.
Massawomeks (Iroquois), 70, 71, 72, 73, 75, 82.
Mascoutins, 155.
Matchedash bay, 33.
Mattawan river, 32, 130.
Mélanges D'Histoire et de Littérature (Sulte) cited, 137.
Merchants of France, a company of, formed in 1603, to prosecute Canadian enterprise, 7.
"Mer Douce" (Fresh Sea — Lake Huron), 32, 104, 140, 155, 159, 160, 161, 162, 163.
Minquas (Southern Iroquois), 79, 150.
Mocosa, ancient name of Virginia, 137.
Mohawk, Indians, 36, 39, 78, 79, 148.

INDEX.

Mohican Indians, 78.
Montreal, 4, 62, 158.
Montreal, island of, discovered by Cartier, 4; in 1603, without inhabitants, 129.
Montagnais, 10, 11, 14, 127.
"Mont Royale," 4, 140.

Narrative and Critical History of America (Winsor) cited, 6, 30, 62, 68, 119, 135, 147, 164.
Nation du Petun (Tobacco nation), 60, 112, 148, 149, 165.
"Nation de l'Isle," 122.
Neill, Rev. Edward D., 147, 158, 160.
Neutrals, 49, 50, 51, 60, 100, 111, 112, 113, 114, 148, 149, 163, 164, 165.
New Amsterdam, 133.
New France, 1, 6, 12, 13, 78, 99, 100, 114, 116, 119.
New Netherland, 78.
Niagara, cataract of, 8, 50, 137, 138, 139, 140.
Niagara river, 8, 49, 50, 51, 76, 94, 111, 113, 143, 164.
Nichols Pond, locality of, 134, 135.
Nicolet, John, 18, 99, 106, 130.
"North Sea," 30, 100, 104, 154, 155.
Nipissing Indians, 32, 44, 60.
North Channel of Lake Huron, 99, 100, 102, 105, 155, 156, 157.
Nottawassaga bay, 33, 60.

Ochastaiguins (Ochatequins), 126.
Ochateguin, a Huron chief, 19, 126, 131.
Ochateguins (Hurons), 15, 126.
"Ogehage" (Minquas), 79.

Oneida Indians, 36, 39, 148.
Oneida lake, 45, 135, 136, 140.
Oneida river, 45.
Onondaga Indians, 36, 37, 38, 39, 46, 54, 58, 59, 90, 148.
Onondaga town (or fort), 46, 53, 59, 60, 80, 81, 133, 134, 135, 136.
Onojutta-Haga Indians, 82, 149.
"Onontiogas" (Carantouannais), 132.
Ontonogan river, 126.
Otis, Charles Pomeroy, 25, 31, 62, 125, 136.
Ottawa river first heard of by Cartier, 4; description of, *ibid.;* mentioned, 14, 20, 27, 32, 33, 48, 62, 96, 97, 100, 130, 155.
Ottawa Indians, 33.
Otoüacha, a Huron town, 34.
Otzinachson Indians, 82, 149.
Orleans, island of, discovered, 3; above it, Quebec is commenced by Champlain, 12.
"Ouendat," see "Wendat."
Ouasouarim Indians, 105.
Oumisagai Indians, 105, 106.
Ounontisaston, a village of the Neutrals, 163, 164.
Outchougai Indians, 105.
Ozinies, 84, 85.

Parkman, Francis, 12, 20, 24, 30, 48, 49, 62, 81, 88, 91, 93, 96, 98, 117, 119, 126, 131, 132, 135, 138, 143, 146, 165.
Patapsco river, 70.
Penetanguishene bay, 129.
Pennsylvania Magazine of History and Biography, extracts from, 52, 64, 95, 120, 132, 135.

"People of the Falls" ("Sauteurs"), 107.
Petun nation, see Tobacco nation.
Pioneers of France in the New World (Parkman) cited, 12, 20, 30, 48, 62, 81, 88, 91, 93, 96, 117, 119, 126, 128, 132, 135, 138, 141, 147, 166.
Prince Edward Island discovered by Cartier, 2.
Prince Society Publications of Champlain's *Voyages*, cited, 23, 25, 31, 38, 47, 62, 63, 68, 102, 104, 119, 125, 126, 127, 135, 138, 141, 143, 147, 150, 151, 152, 158, 271, 274.
Pontgrave, 7, 10, 30.
Potomac river, 70, 82, 146, 149.
Powhatan, 74, 82.
Puants (Winnebago Indians), 159.

Quebec, 8, 10, 12, 26, 108, 114, 116, 117, 118, 119, 130, 133, 150, 166.
"Quebec," signification of, 4.
Quinte bay, 134, 140.

Rapids of St. Louis (Lachine rapids), 114.
Raye, Peter, 118, 152, 166.
Relation des Hurons cited, 123, 166.
Richelieu river, 128, 140.
"River of the Hiroquois" (Niagara river), 113.
Riuière des Puans (Winnebago, now Fox river of Green bay), 159.
Roberval given vice-regal powers over New France, 6.

Sagard, Gabriel, 26, 91, 92, 104, 106, 107, 108, 109, 110, 121, 134, 152, 155, 156, 157, 158, 161, 163.
"Santa Maria," bay of, 68.
"Sasquesahanocks," 74, 75, 82, 83, 84, 144, 145, 146.
Saut de Gaston, 107, 171.
"Sault de Gaston" (Saut de Gaston — Sault Ste. Marie), 159, 162.
"Sault du Gaston," 160.
Sault Ste. Marie, 101, 106, 160, 161.
Saut S. Louis (Lachine rapids), 109.
Sassafras river, 72, 74, 84.
Savignon, a Huron hostage, 18, 19, 21, 22, 23, 131.
Scahentoarruon Indians, 82, 149.
Seneca Indians, 36, 39, 43, 50, 51, 52, 87, 89, 95, 111, 132, 143, 148.
Shea, John Gilmary, 52, 62, 64, 68, 95, 120, 132, 134, 135, 164.
Six Nations Indians, 149.
Slafter, Rev. Edmund F., 25, 30, 31, 47, 62, 63, 68, 102, 126, 127, 132, 135, 138, 141, 143, 147, 150, 151, 158, 159, 162.
Smith, Capt. John, 69, 70, 71, 73, 74, 75, 76, 82, 83, 142, 144, 145, 146.
"Smith's Falls," 144.
Sonnontowans (Senecas), 148.
Southern Iroquois, 79, 82, 85, 148.
St. Charles river, 5.
St. Clair river, 8.
St. Lawrence, bay of, discovered by Cartier, 3.
St. Lawrence river, discovered by Cartier, 3; reaches from Lake Ontario to the gulf, 8;

mentioned, 76, 96, 100, 102, 104, 114, 130, 147.
St. Louis, Falls of (Lachine rapids), 23, 27.
St. Louis river, 8, 157.
St. Mary river, 8, 106.
Sulte, Benjamin, 6, 18, 52, 86, 98, 129, 137, 153, 166.
Susquehannock Indians (Susquehanna Indians), 148, 150.
Susquehanna river, 66, 67, 69, 70, 71, 74, 76, 80, 81, 82, 86, 87, 142, 143, 145, 147; East Branch of, 52; West Branch, 66, 76, 82, 142, 143.

Tadoussac, at mouth of the Saguenay, 7, 8, 18, 100, 114, 116, 117, 127, 129.
Tessouat (Algonquin chief), 129.
Three rivers, 98, 99, 114, 151, 153.
Thwaites, Reuben Gold, 6, 120.
Tioga river, 143.
Tionnontates (Tobacco Nation), 59, 148, 149.
Toanché, 34, 95, 112, 114, 120, 123, 157, 160.

Tobacco Nation (Nation du Petun), 100, 112, 148, 149.
Tockwogh Indians, 72, 73, 75, 82, 83, 84, 145, 146.
Tockwogh river, 72, 73, 74.
Tregouaroti, brother of Savignon, 19, 23, 131.
Trent river, 44, 48.
Tuscarawa Indians, 148, 149.

Verrazzano, John, 1, 68.
Vignau, Nicholas, 24, 27.

"Wendats" (Wyandots — Hurons), 127, 138, 139.
"Wenowances," Susquehanna Indian chiefs, 74.
Western Iroquois, 148.
"Wighcocomicos" (Wicomico Indians), 84.
"Wild Oats" (Menomonee Indians), 157, 161.
Winnebagoes, 155.
Winsor, Justin, 6, 21, 59, 62, 68, 104, 107, 119, 128, 135, 138, 140, 141, 143, 147, 157, 159, 161, 164.
Wyandots, 138, 149.

www.ingramcontent.com/pod-product-compliance
Lightning Source LLC
Chambersburg PA
CBHW020833230426
43666CB00007B/1201